KS3
German

Complete Revision
and Practice

Contents

Contents

Published by CGP

Editors:
Paul Jordin
Jo Sharrock
Hayley Thompson
Rachel Ward

Contributors:
Sheila Brighten
Bettina Hermoso-Gomez
Louise Mycock
Katharine Wright

With thanks to Esther Bond, Miriam Mentel and Glenn Rogers for the proofreading.

Audio CD produced by Naomi Laredo of Small Print and recorded, edited and mastered at The Speech Recording Studio by Graham C. Williams, featuring the voices of Bernd Bauermeister, Felix Hermerschmidt, Nelly Jonsson and Lena Lohmann.

ISBN: 978 1 84762 889 3
Website: www.cgpbooks.co.uk
Printed by Elanders Ltd, Newcastle upon Tyne.
Clipart from CorelDRAW®

Based on the classic CGP style created by Richard Parsons.

Numbers

You can't get out of learning <u>numbers</u>. They're just too darned useful.

Learn the numbers — **die Zahlen**

<u>Practise</u> saying these numbers <u>out loud</u>:

1	2	3	4	5	6	7	8	9	10
eins	zwei	drei	vier	fünf	sechs	sieben	acht	neun	zehn

The words for 13 to 19 all mean "<u>three-ten</u>" etc.
Watch out for 16 and 17 — they're "<u>sechzehn</u>" and "<u>siebzehn</u>".

11	12	13	14	15	16	17	18	19	20
elf	zwölf	dreizehn	vierzehn	fünfzehn	sechzehn	siebzehn	achtzehn	neunzehn	zwanzig

After "<u>dreißig</u>", all the ten-type numbers are pretty easy. You just write the number + "<u>zig</u>" (e.g. "vierzig", "fünfzig"). Watch out for "<u>sechzig</u>" and "<u>siebzig</u>" though.

20	30	40	50	60	70	80	90	100
zwanzig	dreißig	vierzig	fünfzig	sechzig	siebzig	achtzig	neunzig	hundert

The in-betweeners are <u>backwards</u> — say "<u>two and twenty</u>", not "twenty-two".

21	einundzwanzig
22	zweiundzwanzig
23	dreiundzwanzig
24	vierundzwanzig...

Add "te" to a number to get fourth, fifth etc...

Just get the number and bung on "<u>te</u>". You need these for saying "<u>third</u> of November", "<u>first</u> on the left" etc. Watch out for 1st, 3rd, 7th and 8th though, as they're a bit different.

1st	2nd	3rd	4th	5th	6th	7th	8th
erste	zweite	dritte	vierte	fünfte	sechste	siebte	achte

For numbers from <u>20</u> to <u>100</u>, add "<u>ste</u>", e.g. zwanzig<u>ste</u>, einundreißig<u>ste</u>.

There's really no choice — you've got to learn these numbers

There are no shortcuts here — you just have to say the numbers to yourself over and over again. They're used in so many different topics, you'll be glad you know them. Really.

Time

You don't just get to <u>learn</u> numbers — you actually get to <u>use</u> them. This page is all about time.

Learn all the **clock times**

Swap the highlighted numbers for any number from page 1 to make the different times.

1) THE O'CLOCKS

sieben Uhr = <u>seven</u> o'clock

ein Uhr = <u>one</u> o'clock

For one o'clock, you say "ein" (not "eins").

2) QUARTER TO AND QUARTER PAST

Viertel vor sieben = quarter to <u>seven</u>

Viertel nach sieben = quarter past <u>seven</u>

You don't need to say "Uhr" for these.

3) MINUTES TO AND MINUTES PAST

fünf vor sieben = <u>five</u> to <u>seven</u>

fünf nach sieben = <u>five</u> past <u>seven</u>

4) HALF ~~PAST~~ TO

halb sieben = half to <u>seven</u> (half past six)

halb acht = half to <u>eight</u> (half past seven)

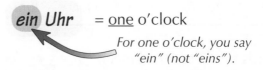

Weird this one — "halb sieben" means half <u>to</u> seven, i.e. half past six. Don't get caught out.

5) AT + TIME

um sieben Uhr = at <u>seven</u> o'clock

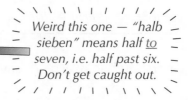

NB — Germans use the 24-hour clock a lot.
4 am is 04:00 — vier Uhr.
4 pm is 16:00 — sechzehn Uhr.

What time is it? — **Wie spät ist es?**

Wie viel Uhr ist es?

OR

Wie spät ist es?

= What time is it?

Es ist + TIME

Es ist drei Uhr. = It's <u>three</u> o'clock.

Remember 'halb sieben' means 'half <u>to</u> seven'

That "half to seven" stuff is weird, but it really is how you do it in German.
Make sure you've got it sussed or you'll be an hour late for everything and feel a little bit silly.

Times and Dates

Time isn't all about clocks — you also need to know times of day.

Other times — today, tomorrow, evening...

Learn these words for <u>chunks of time</u>. They're useful for saying <u>roughly</u> when things happen.

gestern = yesterday

heute = today

morgen = tomorrow

Watch out for "morgen" and "der Morgen" — they mean different things.

der Morgen / Vormittag = morning

der Nachmittag = afternoon

der Abend = evening

die Nacht = night

der Tag = day

die Woche = week

der Monat = month

das Jahr = year

The **days** of the week

Seven days, seven bits of vocab...

Montag	**Dienstag**	**Mittwoch**	**Donnerstag**	**Freitag**
Monday	Tuesday	Wednesday	Thursday	Friday

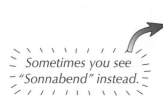
Sometimes you see "Sonnabend" instead.

Samstag	**Sonntag**	**das Wochenende**
Saturday	Sunday	weekend

To say, e.g. "on Monday<u>s</u>", you put the first letter of the day in <u>lower case</u> and add "<u>s</u>":

Ich schlafe montags. = I sleep on <u>Mondays</u>.

To say, e.g. "on Monday", you put "<u>am</u>" + the day:

Gehen wir am Montag. = Let's go on <u>Monday</u>.

Maybe not today, maybe not tomorrow...

Some of the days are similar in English and German, and there are only seven of them, so there's no excuse not to learn them. Cover up the German and see if you know them already.

Dates

And some more vocab. The months aren't <u>too</u> bad — they're not that different from the English.

Months of the year

Learn them in these <u>groups of four</u>. They look pretty much like the English months — but look closely at the <u>spellings</u>.

Januar January	*Februar* February	*März* March	*April* April
Mai May	*Juni* June	*Juli* July	*August* August
September September	*Oktober* October	*November* November	*Dezember* December

Talking about dates

You need dates for <u>booking holidays</u> (p.92) and <u>saying when your birthday is</u> (p.14).

To give the date when something will happen, start off with "<u>am</u>".
Then get the word for "first", "second" etc. from the bottom of p.1 and add "<u>n</u>".

am neunten *April*   = on the <u>ninth</u> of April

am zwölften *August*   = on the <u>twelfth</u> of August

The "n" is because it's dative.
See p.114 if you're interested.

If you want to do a date that's "<u>20th</u>" or above, don't forget the extra "<u>s</u>":

am zwanzigsten *Mai*   = on the <u>twentieth</u> of May

I'm always happy 'am fünfundzwanzigsten Dezember'

Write out the months in English and translate them — then translate them back. Do the same with them in a random order — this'll make sure you really know each of 'em, not just the list.

Practice Questions

Track 1   Listening Question

1   Listen to the six times mentioned in German, then write down the number of the matching clock face (1-6). For example, the first answer is clock 4.

1    2    3

4    5    6

2   Match the German words to numbers from the box.

a) dreiundsiebzig
b) zweiundneunzig
c) zwölf
d) einunddreißig
e) fünfundzwanzig
f) sechsundachtzig
g) drei
h) zehn
i) fünf
j) sechzehn

31 92 25 86 3 10 12 16 5 73

3   Translate these German expressions of time into English.

a) morgen   c) Abend   e) Nachmittag
b) Woche   d) Monat   f) Tag

4   Write out these dates as words in German. I've done the first one for you.

a) on the thirty-first of December   *am einunddreißigsten Dezember*
b) on the sixteenth of April
c) on the first of July
d) on the twenty-eighth of February
e) on the third of September
f) on the twenty-ninth of May

Meeting and Greeting

Normally, <u>hello</u> is the first thing you say, but I decided to leave it till <u>page 6</u>.

Saying hello — Guten Tag

The first thing you'll hear or say is one of these <u>greetings</u>.
Learn these ice-breakers and when to use which one.

1)   There are <u>two general ones</u>:

Guten Tag   = Hello   ⬅   Quite <u>formal</u>. Literally means 'good day'.

Hallo   = Hi   ⬅   Less formal, i.e. you'd say it to your <u>mates</u>.

2)   There are also specific hello words for <u>different times</u> of the day:

Guten Morgen   = Good morning

Guten Abend   = Good evening   **Gute Nacht**   = Good night

3)   You can say hello words either on their own, or with a <u>name</u>.
     E.g. Guten Morgen, Daniela / Guten Tag, Herr Schröder / Hallo Thomas etc...

Saying goodbye — Auf Wiedersehen

You should use a <u>formal goodbye</u> for <u>older people</u> and <u>strangers</u>. Use the <u>informal</u>
ones for your <u>mates</u> or people your <u>own age</u>. But if in doubt, go for formal.

Auf Wiedersehen   = Goodbye

This is a bit <u>formal</u> — it literally means 'until we see each other again'.

Both of these are <u>more casual</u>:   **Tschüss**   = Bye

Bis später   = See you later

You can't get away with not learning this
It's pretty important to be able to say hello and goodbye, but make sure you know which
version to use. The queen might be annoyed if you greet her with 'Hallo' and not 'Guten Tag'.

Meeting and Greeting

Lots more useful phrases for when you first <u>meet</u> people... Manners cost nothing etc.

Introducing people — Darf ich ... vorstellen?

Sometimes you might have to <u>introduce</u> someone. You can use either of these two ways.

Darf ich Ihnen Stefan vorstellen? = May I introduce <u>you</u> to <u>Stefan</u>?

Swap "Ihnen" for "<u>dir</u>" if you're speaking to someone your age or younger.
Swap "Ihnen" for "<u>euch</u>" if you're speaking to more than one person your age or younger.

Darf ich Ihnen meinen Freund vorstellen? Er heißt Stefan.

= May I introduce you to <u>my friend</u>? <u>He</u> is called <u>Stefan</u>.

If you're introducing a girl or woman, say "mei<u>ne</u> Freund<u>in</u>", and "<u>sie</u> heißt".

Pleased to meet you

When <u>you've</u> been introduced, reply with "pleased to meet you".

Schön, Sie kennen zu lernen. = Pleased to meet you.

Swap "Sie" for "<u>dich</u>" if you're speaking to someone your age or younger.

How are you? — Wie geht es dir?

These phrases all mean '<u>How are you?</u>'.

(1) **Wie geht es dir?**

(2) **Wie geht's?**
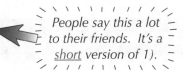
People say this a lot to their friends. It's a <u>short</u> version of 1).

(3) **Wie geht es Ihnen?**

This is the <u>formal</u> version.

Here's what you could <u>answer</u>: **Gut, danke.** = I'm well, thanks.

Practise introducing people to your friends and parents

In the UK you normally say "This is Kevin." Then everybody says "Alright Kevin." And that's it.
German-speakers are a little bit more formal, so you need all this manners-type vocab.

Being Polite

This page contains some really important phrases, so you'd best get learning them.

Please and thank you — bitte, danke

You don't want to go round <u>winding people up</u> — learn how to say please and thank you.

bitte = please

danke = thank you / thanks

danke schön = thank you very much

Yes, no — ja, nein

If somebody asks you if you want something you could just answer with "yes" or "no":

ja = yes   *nein* = no

But obviously it's loads <u>better</u> to say "Yes, please," or "No, thank you."

Ja, bitte. = Yes, please.   *Nein, danke.* = No, thanks.

You're welcome — bitte schön

You hear this <u>everywhere</u>. Shop assistants probably say it about a thousand times a day.

Sometimes people just say "bitte".   *bitte schön* = you're welcome

---

Please learn these phrases — thank you very much

These are the basic must-have bits of German. If you learn nothing else, learn these words and how to spell them. Then practise adding 'bitte' and 'danke' to your sentences.

Being Polite

It's the same in any language — saying "I want chips" doesn't work, but "Could I have a bag of chips, please?" works wonders. This page is about saying "I would like" <u>rather than</u> "I want".

I would like... — Ich möchte...

1) "I would like" (<u>ich möchte</u>) is polite. "I want" (<u>ich will</u>) is dead rude.

Ich möchte einen Kuchen. = I would like a cake.

2) You can also say you'd like <u>to do</u> something:

Ich möchte + VERB → *The verb has to be in the <u>infinitive</u> form — see p.123.*

Ich möchte singen. = I would like <u>to sing</u>.

to play football: Fußball spielen
to go out: ausgehen

May I...? — Darf ich...?

Be polite by <u>asking permission</u> to do things. This is the special <u>rule</u> for saying 'May I...?':

Darf ich + INFINITIVE

Darf ich ein Brötchen haben, bitte? *Haben and singen are <u>infinitives</u> — see p.123.*

= May I have a roll, please?

Darf ich singen, bitte?

= May I sing, please?

Remember 'I want' = bad, 'I would like' = good

There are tons of variations for the "I would like" and "May I" sentences — learn all the examples here, and write out at least five more of your own. Don't forget about the infinitive.

Being Polite

And now you need to learn how to say 'sorry' and 'excuse me'.

Get yourself off the hook — say **sorry** and **excuse me**

Learn this <u>phrase</u> for "I'm sorry":

> ***es tut mir leid***   = I'm sorry

> ***Es tut mir leid, aber ich mag Käse nicht.***
>
>> = I'm sorry, but I don't like cheese.

This is how you say "<u>excuse me</u>" politely:

> ***entschuldigen Sie***   = excuse me

> ***Entschuldigen Sie, wo ist das Kino bitte?***
>
>> = Excuse me, where is the cinema please?

Offer to **help**, and **don't upset people**

1)   Ask if you can <u>help</u> — it makes you look good. (See p.27 for more chores.)

> ***Soll ich das Essen zubereiten ?***   = Should I <u>prepare the meal</u>?

> *lay the table:* den Tisch decken
> *do the washing-up:* spülen

2)   If you're going to say something you think <u>they won't like</u>, start with "es tut mir leid":

> ***Es tut mir leid, aber ich esse kein Fleisch.***
>
>> = I'm sorry, but I don't eat meat.

Es tut mir leid, but you really need to know this stuff

Learning these few phrases will keep everyone happy. Just make sure you know what the phrases mean as well — otherwise you won't know which chore you've offered to help with.

Practice Questions

Track 2   Listening Question

1 Listen to these conversations, then write down whether the statement for each conversation is true or false.

a) This is an informal conversation.

b) This is a formal conversation.

c) Susanna is offering to cook dinner.

d) Flora doesn't want a coffee.

2 Read these situations and write the most appropriate hello/goodbye phrase for each one. Don't use the same phrase twice. I've done the first one for you.

a) You've been to the cinema with some German mates and now you're all going home.   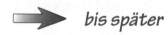 *bis später*

b) You greet your German penpal's parents when you arrive home for dinner after 5 p.m.

c) Time for bed. What are you going to say to your penpal's family?

d) It's 9 a.m. the next morning and you want to buy a drink at the shop. How do you greet the shopkeeper?

e) You meet your German mates at the local shopping centre the next day. What do you say to them when you first see them?

f) You see your penpal's teacher out shopping at 1 p.m. Be polite and greet him.

g) You're at the airport about to leave Germany now. Time to say goodbye to your penpal's parents.

h) Now you're saying goodbye to your German penpal at the airport. What do you say?

Practice Questions

3 Read the situations on the left and match each one to the most appropriate German sentence on the right. Use each sentence once.

1. You're introducing Bernd to your German teacher.

2. You're introducing a female friend to your penpal's parents.

3. You're introducing Bernd to your younger brother and his friends.

4. You're introducing Bernd to your best friend who's the same age as you.

a. Darf ich dir Bernd vorstellen?

b. Darf ich euch Bernd vorstellen?

c. Darf ich Ihnen Bernd vorstellen?

d. Darf ich Ihnen meine Freundin vorstellen?

4 Copy and complete these sentences using the words from the box.

a) Gut, ...

b) Wie geht es .... ?

c) Wie .... ?

d) Wie .... es Ihnen?

e) .... , Sie kennen zu lernen.

> danke
> dir
> schön
> geht's
> geht

5 Write these German phrases out in English. Choose from the phrases in the box.

a) Ich will   c) Ich möchte   e) danke schön

b) bitte   d) Darf ich   f) bitte schön

> thank you very much
> May I
> I would like
> please
> I want
> you're welcome

6 Rewrite these sentences to make them polite. I've done the first one for you.

a) You would like an apple.
    DON'T SAY: "Ich will einen Apfel." BE POLITE *Ich möchte einen Apfel.*

b) You would like to sit here.
    DON'T SAY: "Ich will hier sitzen." BE POLITE

c) You would like a bread roll.
    DON'T SAY: "Ich will ein Brötchen." BE POLITE

d) You would like to do the washing up.
    DON'T SAY: "Ich will spülen." BE POLITE

Summary Questions

Congratulations, you've reached the end of the section. Now you get to test what you've learnt and what you've forgotten by trying to answer these questions. If you don't know the answer, look back through the section to find it. Then learn it and try the question again.

1) Count to ten in German.

2) Count backwards from ten to one in German.

3) Count to twenty in German — out loud.

4) Write down the German for these numbers: *(in words, not numbers)*
   a) 17   b) 23   c) 38   d) 64   e) 100

5) Write down your house number in German.

6) Write down the number of people in your German class in German.

7) Translate these words into German, and write them out in words:
   a) first   b) third   c) seventh   d) eighth   e) ninth

8) Write out all these times in German, in words:
   a) 09:00   b) 10:10   c) 11:15   d) 12:40   e) 13:30   f) 14:45

9) Translate this fascinating conversation:
   "Wie viel Uhr ist es?"   *"Es ist Viertel vor fünf."*

10) Answer this question in German:
    "Wie spät ist es?"

11) Put these time words in size order, with the one that lasts longest first.
    der Tag   das Jahr   der Monat   die Woche

12) Write down "der", "die" or "das" for each of these words:
    Morgen   Nachmittag   Abend   Nacht

13) Write down the days of the week in German.

14) Which of these phrases would you be likely to use with people your own age?
    a) Guten Tag   b) Hallo   c) Auf Wiedersehen   d) Tschüss

15) Roughly, what time of day would it be if somebody said "Guten Abend" to you?

16) You're out in town with your German penfriend and you run into someone she knows.
    She says: *"Darf ich dir Clothilde vorstellen?"* What does it mean?

17) How do you say "Pleased to meet you", in German?

18) Write down three different ways of saying "How are you?" in German.

19) How do you say "Yes, please" and "No, thanks"?

20) Which of these sounds more polite?
    "Ich möchte Elefanten."   or   *"Ich will Elefanten."*

21) You've accidentally trodden on the Chancellor's grandma's ingrowing toenail.
    What do you say?

22) Write this out in German.
    "Should I wash the car?"

Your Details

This section mostly involves telling people about yourself. Shouldn't be too hard...

Talking about yourself — **facts and figures**

You need to know these <u>four questions</u>, and how to <u>answer</u> them.
Customise the answers to fit <u>you</u>, by changing the <u>underlined</u> bits.

① **Wie heißt du?**   = What are you called?

Ich heiße <u>Sheila</u>.   = I'm called <u>Sheila</u>.

② **Wie alt bist du?**   = How old are you?

Ich bin <u>vierzehn</u> Jahre alt.   = I'm <u>fourteen</u>.

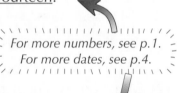

For more numbers, see p.1.
For more dates, see p.4.

③ **Wann hast du Geburtstag?**   = When is your birthday?

Ich habe am <u>vierten Juli</u> Geburtstag.   = My birthday is on the <u>4th of July</u>.

④ **Was magst du?**   = What do you like?

Ich mag <u>Schokolade</u>.   = I like <u>chocolate</u>.

For other ways of saying what
you like and don't like, see p.99.

Make sure you can give answers to all of these questions

It's all great stuff for a first letter to a penpal and pretty useful for whenever you meet someone new. Make sure you learn the birthday bit, or there's no way of dropping hints.

Your Details

And now you get to describe your beautiful looks and great personality...

Say what you **look like**

You need to be able to describe how you look — that means talking about your eyes, height, hair, glasses...

Ich habe grüne Augen. = I have <u>green</u> eyes.

green: grüne
blue: blaue
brown: braune

Ich bin klein. = I am <u>short</u>.

small, short: klein   fat: dick
tall: groß   thin: dünn
medium height: mittelgroß   slim: schlank

Ich habe blonde Haare. = I have <u>blonde</u> hair.

blonde: blonde
black: schwarze
brown: braune
red: rote

short: kurze
long: lange
shoulder-length: schulterlange
quite long: relativ lange

Ich trage eine Brille. = I wear glasses.

Ich trage keine Brille. = I don't wear glasses.

Describe your **personality**

Ich bin faul. = I am <u>lazy</u>.

hardworking: fleißig
sporty: sportlich
shy: schüchtern
nice: nett

Learn this stuff off by heart

This is pretty straightforward stuff and you should be able to trot it out without too much worry. Plus if you learn this stuff now, it'll make your life much easier when it comes to page 17.

Your Family

A lot of these German words <u>sound</u> a bit like the English, so they're not too tricky to remember.

Use these words for your **friends** and **family**

my father:
mein Vater

my sister:
meine Schwester

my brother:
mein Bruder

my mother:
meine Mutter

my friend:
meine Freundin

my grandfather:
mein Großvater

my grandmother:
meine Großmutter

my friend:
mein Freund

my aunt:
meine Tante

my uncle:
mein Onkel

STEP STUFF

my stepfather: mein Stiefvater
my stepmother: meine Stiefmutter
my stepbrother: mein Stiefbruder
my stepsister: meine Stiefschwester

my cousin (male):
mein Cousin

my cousin (female):
meine Cousine

Cover up the German, write it out, then check if it's right

Now's the time when it's useful to have a small family. See if you can remember the German words for all your relations. And don't mix up your grandmother and grandfather.

Your Family

As well as talking about yourself you also need to be able to talk about your family...

Say what your **family** and **friends** are **like**

Use these phrases to describe your <u>friends</u> and <u>family</u> (swap Bruder/Schwester for anyone you want). The phrases are slightly <u>different</u> for <u>lads</u> or <u>lasses</u> (see those underlined bits), so I've written them out twice.

PHRASES ABOUT LADS	**PHRASES ABOUT LASSES**

Ich habe <u>einen</u> Bruder.

= I have a <u>brother</u>.

Ich habe <u>eine</u> Schwester.

= I have a <u>sister</u>.

<u>Mein</u> Bruder heißt John.

= My <u>brother</u> is called <u>John</u>.

<u>Meine</u> Schwester heißt Louise.

= My <u>sister</u> is called <u>Louise</u>.

<u>Er</u> ist elf Jahre alt.

= He's <u>eleven</u> years old.

<u>Sie</u> ist elf Jahre alt.

= She's <u>eleven</u> years old.

<u>Er</u> ist nett.

= He's <u>nice</u>.

<u>Sie</u> ist nett.

= She's <u>nice</u>.

If you're an only child...

Here's what you need to say if you're an only child:

Ich bin ein Einzelkind.   = I am an only child.

If only I were an only child

You can use these few phrases to describe everyone in your family. You might want to look on p.15 for some more descriptive words — no one will believe you if you say everyone is 'nice'.

Pets and Animals

If you don't have a pet, you could just <u>pretend</u> you do. It might be a lie, but it'll help you learn <u>German</u> and it might be fun to own a cow called Ethel.

Learn the pets — die Haustiere

Don't just learn each animal name — learn if it's "<u>der</u>", "<u>die</u>" or "<u>das</u>" as well.

bird:
der Vogel

horse:
das Pferd

cow:
die Kuh

dog:
der Hund

rabbit:
das Kaninchen

cat:
die Katze

hamster:
der Hamster

mouse:
die Maus

tortoise:
die Schildkröte

Make sure you learn <u>all</u> of these animals

You might not have any pets, but if someone else tells you about theirs it could get embarrassing if you thought their dog was a hedgehog. By the way, hedgehog is "der Igel".

Pets and Animals

As well as describing yourself and your family, you also need to be able to describe your pets — even if they're made up. I have a cow called Ethel. She is big and sweet.

I have a hamster — Ich habe einen Hamster

You need to <u>understand</u> people talking about <u>their pets</u>, and talk about <u>yours</u> if you have one. I've used "Hamster" as an example — swap in the word for the pet you want to talk about.

① **Ich habe einen Hamster.**   = I have <u>a hamster</u>.

It's "einen" for "der" animals, but "eine" for "die" ones, and "ein" for "das" ones (see p.113).

② **Mein Hamster heißt 'Killer'.**   = <u>My hamster</u> is called 'Killer'.

It's "mein" for "der" animals, but "meine" for "die" ones, and "mein" for "das" ones (see p.107).

③ **Ich habe keine Haustiere.**   = I don't have any pets.

④ **Mein Hamster ist süß.**   = <u>My hamster</u> is <u>sweet</u>.

nasty: böse
big: groß
black: schwarz

Don't forget to check if your pet is "der", "die" or "das"

If you want to go into more fascinating detail about your pet, see: page 15 for the word "small" (and for some more personality types) and page 62 for other colours. Great. Onwards...

Practice Questions

Track 3   Listening Question

1   Listen to Wilhelm talking about himself and his family.
    Answer the following questions.

    a)   How many people live in Wilhelm's house?

    b)   Who is Kirsten?

    c)   What colour eyes has Wilhelm's father got?

    d)   How does Wilhelm describe his brother?

2   Match the German sentences on the left with their English meanings on the right.

    1. Ich habe am dritten Mai Geburtstag.   a. I like football.

    2. Was magst du?   b. I'm called Aleesha.

    3. Ich heiße Aleesha.   c. What are you called?

    4. Ich bin neunzehn Jahre alt.   d. My birthday is on the 3rd of May.

    5. Wie heißt du?   e. When is your birthday?

    6. Ich mag Fußball.   f. I am nineteen.

    7. Wie alt bist du?   g. How old are you?

    8. Wann hast du Geburtstag?   h. What do you like?

3   George has had a letter from his new German penpal Peter.
    Read the letter, then write down if the statements below are true or false.

    Lieber George,

    Ich heiße Peter. Ich bin fünfzehn
    Jahre alt. Ich habe am ersten Oktober
    Geburtstag. Ich mag Fußball und
    Tennis. Ich bin klein und dünn.
    Ich habe braune Augen und ich trage
    eine Brille. Ich habe blonde Haare.

    Peter

    a)   Peter says he is fourteen.

    b)   His birthday is on the 3rd of October.

    c)   He likes tennis.

    d)   He has brown eyes.

    e)   He doesn't wear glasses.

    f)   He has blond hair.

Practice Questions

4 Copy out Petra's family tree and fill in the missing bits. Each missing bit should say "my mother", "my cousin" etc. in German. Two have been done for you.

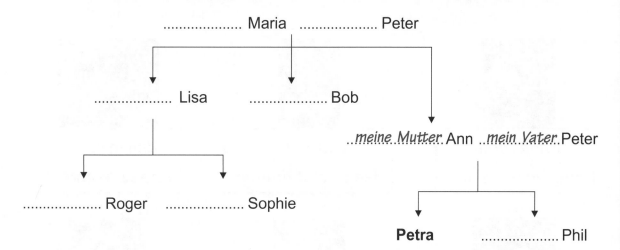

.... Maria .... Peter

.... Lisa .... Bob

meine Mutter Ann *mein Vater* Peter

.... Roger .... Sophie

Petra .... Phil

5 Write down the German word for each of these beasts, including the **der**, **die** or **das**.

a)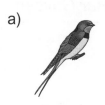

c)

e)

b)

d)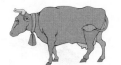

f)

6 Sort these words out to make sentences about pets. The first one has been done for you.

a) keine Haustiere habe ich
   Ich habe keine Haustiere.

b) Kaninchen habe ein ich

c) einen hat sie Hamster

d) hast du eine Katze

e) ist Hund mein böse

f) Schildkröte "Speedy" meine heißt

22

Your Home

And now some more words to learn — this time you need to be able to describe your house.

Talk about the **rooms** in your house — **die Zimmer**

['das Zimmer' = room]

living room:
das Wohnzimmer

bedroom:
das Schlafzimmer

dining room:
das Esszimmer

bathroom:
das Badezimmer

kitchen:
die Küche

garden:
der Garten

At home — **zu Hause**

Was für ein Haus hast du?   = What's your house like?

Zu Hause gibt es fünf *Zimmer.*

= In my home, there are <u>five</u> rooms.

Change the bits in green so they match your home. See p.1 for more numbers.

Zu Hause gibt es eine Küche und zwei Schlafzimmer*.*

= In my home, there is <u>a kitchen and two bedrooms</u>.

The bit after "es gibt / gibt es" is accusative, so it's einen for "der" words, eine for "die", and ein for "das" words (see p.112).

You should be able to say what rooms are in your house

Use the pictures of the rooms to test if you've learnt the vocab — use strips of paper to cover up the German, then from the pictures, write down the German names for the rooms.

SECTION TWO — YOU, FAMILY AND HOME

Your Home

Empty rooms wouldn't be much fun, so you need to be able to describe the furniture as well.

Talk about the furniture — die Möbel

Learn the words for these pieces of furniture:

bed:
das Bett

sofa:
das Sofa

chair:
der Stuhl

table:
der Tisch

cupboard:
der Schrank

wardrobe:
der Kleiderschrank

In your room — In deinem Schlafzimmer

Learn this question, and how to answer it. Change the green box to make it match your room — choose from the furniture above. And remember — it's einen for "der", eine for "die", and ein for "das" words.

Was für Möbel gibt es in deinem Schlafzimmer?

= What furniture is there in your bedroom?

Es gibt ein Bett und einen Stuhl.

= There is a bed and a chair.

Make sure you know whether to use "ein", "eine" or "einen"

Furniture's not the most interesting thing to talk about, but just in case someone asks you what's in your room, you'd better learn these words. And don't forget to learn the "der", "die" or "das" part.

Where You Live

This is describing <u>whereabouts</u> your home is. It's all good <u>Key Stage Three German</u> stuff...

Tell them where you live — **Ich wohne...**

① Say if you live in a <u>flat</u> or a <u>house</u>...

Ich wohne in...

= I live in...

a flat:
einer Wohnung

a house:
einem Haus

② ...and if you live in a <u>village</u>, <u>town</u> or <u>city</u>.

Ich wohne in...

= I live in...

a village:
einem Dorf

a town:
einer Stadt

a big town / city:
einer Großstadt

You usually use the dative case after "in" — that's why it's "einem" and "einer". See p.114 for more.

Some extra phrases

Ich lebe auf dem Land. = I live in the countryside.

"Ich lebe" is another way of saying "I live".

Ich wohne in den Bergen. = I live in the mountains.

Ich wohne am Meer. = I live at the seaside.

Ich wohne in einem Haus in einem Dorf

People are always interested in where you live, so make sure you learn these phrases. You can combine them to give lots of information — for example, "I live in a house in a village".

Where You Live

Tell them which part of the country you live in

Work out the version of this phrase that you need, and learn it off by heart.

Put the name of where you live in here.

Scotland: Schottland
Wales: Wales
Nordirland: Northern Ireland

Ich wohne in Oxford, einer Stadt in Südengland.

= I live in Oxford, a town in the south of England.

a village: einem Dorf
a town: einer Stadt
a big town/city: einer Großstadt

north: Nord
northwest: Nordwest
northeast: Nordost
west: West
east: Ost
southwest: Südwest
south: Süd
southeast: Südost

Do you like living here? — Lebst du gern hier?

Saying what you think about where you live will help you get your German to a higher level.

Ich lebe gern hier...

= I like living here...

Ich lebe nicht gern hier...

= I don't like living here...

...weil es fantastisch ist.

= ...because it's fantastic.

interesting: interessant
quiet: ruhig

...weil es furchtbar ist.

= ...because it's terrible.

boring: langweilig
too quiet: zu ruhig

For more on using "weil" in a sentence, see p.141.

Look at a map and work out exactly where you live

Being able to give an opinion about things is really useful, especially if you can give a reason for your opinion too. Try saying what you like or don't like about where you live.

Daily Routine

Here's a page about daily routine. If you want daily routine, this is your page...

Daily routine — say what you do

You need to know <u>all these bits</u>. Read them carefully and check out the <u>spellings</u>.

Ich wache auf. = I wake up.

Ich stehe auf. = I get up.

Ich wasche mich. = I wash myself.

Ich putze mir die Zähne. = I brush my teeth.

Ich ziehe mich an. = I get dressed.

Ich esse Frühstück. = I eat breakfast.

Ich gehe zu Fuß zur Schule. = I walk to school.

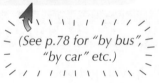
(See p.78 for "by bus", "by car" etc.)

Ich gehe nach Hause. = I go home.

Ich mache meine Hausaufgaben. = I do my homework.

Ich sehe fern. = I watch telly.

Ich esse Abendessen. = I eat dinner.

Ich gehe ins Bett. = I go to bed.

Stick to the routine and learn all of these phrases

Check you've got it all sussed by covering up the German phrases with some paper, and writing them out. Then check you got them all right. If not, read through it all and try again.

Chores

For some reason, you have to talk about what chores you do at home.
This stuff is good for offering to help as well (see p.10).

Learn the **nine** chores

Not that "doing nothing" really counts as a chore. Pity.

Machst du Hausarbeit?

= Do you do any housework?

I go shopping:
Ich gehe einkaufen.

I do the vacuum cleaning:
Ich sauge Staub.

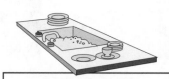

I wash the dishes:
Ich spüle.

I make my bed:
Ich mache mein Bett.

I lay the table:
Ich decke den Tisch.

I don't do anything:
Ich mache nichts.

I clean:
Ich putze.

I wash the car:
Ich wasche das Auto.

I tidy my room:
Ich räume mein Zimmer auf.

Housework — almost as bad as homework

Even if you don't have to do any housework, you still need to know these phrases.
It's not very exciting stuff but it's important that you learn it.

Practice Questions

　　　　　Listening Questions

1　Listen to these four people (a-d) talking about where they live.
Match each person to the correct picture.

1 　　　　2

3 　　　　4

Track 5

2　Listen to Carola talking about her daily routine, then answer these questions.

　a)　At what time does Carola get up?

　b)　Where does she have breakfast?

　c)　What does she have to do before she goes to school?

　d)　What does her brother do every evening?

　e)　What is his opinion of this?

3　Match the English words on the left to the German ones on the right.

　　1. kitchen　　　　　　a.　das Schlafzimmer

　　2. dining room　　　　b.　die Küche

　　3. living room　　　　c.　das Wohnzimmer

　　4. bedroom　　　　　d.　das Badezimmer

　　5. garden　　　　　　e.　der Garten

　　6. bathroom　　　　　f.　das Esszimmer

Practice Questions

4 Copy and complete these sentences, using the words from the box below to fill in the blanks. Use each word once.

a) Zu Hause, gibt es .... Schlafzimmer.

b) Was für ein .... hast du?

c) .... Hause, gibt es eine ....

d) .... für ein Haus hast du?

e) Zu Hause, ... es ein Wohnzimmer.

f) Zu Hause, gibt .... zwei Wohnzimmer.

| Was | gibt | Zu | ein | es | Haus | Küche |

5 Write these sentences out **in English**.

a) Ich wohne in einer Großstadt.

b) Ich wohne in einem Haus.

c) Ich lebe auf dem Land.

d) Ich wohne am Meer.

e) Ich wohne in einem Dorf.

6 Write these out in German:

a) I wash myself.

b) I watch telly.

c) I do my homework.

d) I get dressed.

e) I go to bed.

f) I walk to school.

g) I get up.

h) I eat breakfast.

7 Put the following words in the correct order so that you can make a sentence about "chores". The first one has been done for you.

a) wasche Auto Ich das
   Ich wasche das Auto.

b) decke den Ich Tisch

c) mache Ich Bett mein

d) putze Ich

e) Staub Ich sauge

f) Zimmer räume auf mein Ich

The Body

You need to know the <u>body parts</u> for telling people <u>something hurts</u> (see page 32).

The head — **der Kopf**

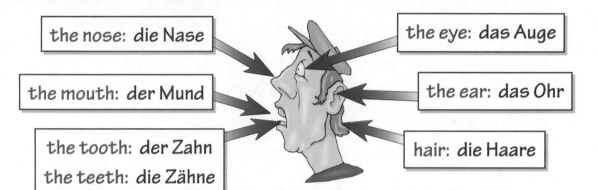

the nose: die Nase

the mouth: der Mund

the tooth: der Zahn
the teeth: die Zähne

the eye: das Auge

the ear: das Ohr

hair: die Haare

The body — **der Körper**

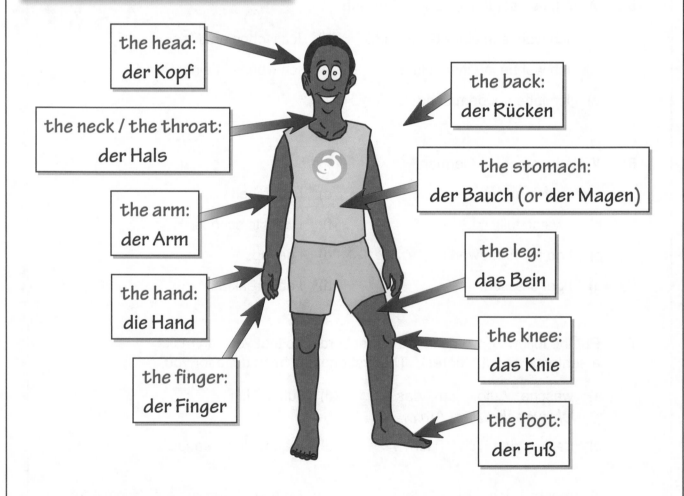

the head: der Kopf

the neck / the throat: der Hals

the arm: der Arm

the hand: die Hand

the finger: der Finger

the back: der Rücken

the stomach: der Bauch (or der Magen)

the leg: das Bein

the knee: das Knie

the foot: der Fuß

Don't just point to where it hurts — learn the words for the body parts

Come on, some of these aren't hard at all — like "die Hand", "der Finger", "der Arm". You're halfway there without even trying. All you have to remember is whether they're der, die or das.

Health and Illness

Being ill <u>sucks</u>. Don't suffer in silence — learn this German and get <u>made better</u> ASAP.

Say that you're ill — Ich bin krank

First you need to say that you're ill, then say where you want to go to get better.

Ich bin krank. = I am ill.

Ich will zum Arzt gehen. = I want to go <u>to the doctor's</u>.

to the hospital: ins Krankenhaus
to the pharmacy: zur Apotheke

Learn these **things** for **making you better**

If you're ill, you'll need one of these things to <u>make you better</u>.

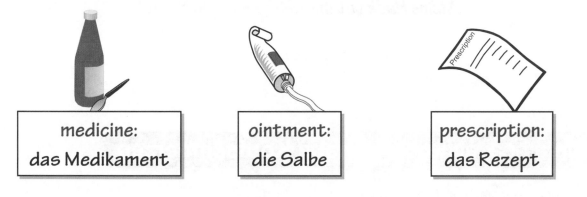

medicine:
das Medikament

ointment:
die Salbe

prescription:
das Rezept

plaster:
das Pflaster

tablet:
die Tablette

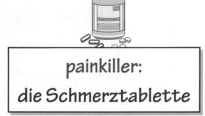

painkiller:
die Schmerztablette

This stuff could actually save your life

'I want to go to the hospital' is a very useful phrase. The others are pretty handy too, so make sure you've learnt them all. You know how to do it — cover, write, check. Easy.

Health and Illness

Being able to say you're ill is useful, but it's more useful to be able to say exactly what hurts.

My leg hurts — Mein Bein tut mir weh

This is how you say what bit of you <u>hurts</u>. Practise bunging in the <u>body parts</u> from page 30.

"mein / meine" + BODY PART + "tut mir weh"

Mein Bein tut mir weh.

= My leg hurts.

It's "mein" for "der" and "das" words, and "meine" for "die" words. See p.107 for more.

Mein Fuß tut mir weh. = My foot hurts.

Meine Hand tut mir weh. = My hand hurts.

Meine Nase tut mir weh. = My nose hurts.

Mein Kopf tut mir weh. = My head hurts.

I have a headache — Ich habe Kopfschmerzen

For your <u>head</u>, <u>stomach</u> and <u>ear</u>, you can say they hurt
or you can use the special "ache" words, like this:

Ich habe Kopfschmerzen. = I have a <u>headache</u>.

stomach ache: Bauchschmerzen
earache: Ohrenschmerzen

Hopefully you won't need these phrases — but learn them anyway

You'll be grateful for this when you finish banging your head against a wall.
You can make yourself a sign saying "ich habe Kopfschmerzen" or "mein Kopf tut mir weh".

Practice Questions

Track 6   Listening Questions

Listen to these conversations between patients and a doctor.
For each statement below, write down whether it is true or false.

1   a)   Frau Reinhard has been ill for a week.

b)   She has a sore throat.

2   a)   Herr Brand has a sore knee.

b)   He has to use the ointment 5 times a day.

3   a)   Susanna has stomach ache.

b)   Susanna is not happy with the doctor's advice.

4   Write out the German for the different
parts of Peter's head. Remember to write
"der", "das" or "die" in front of the word.

5   Write these out in German.
Don't forget the **der**, **die** or **das**.

a)   the knee   d)   the finger

b)   the leg   e)   the stomach

c)   the back   f)   the throat

6   Match the English on the left to the German on the right.

1. pharmacy   a. das Krankenhaus

2. hospital   b. Ich will zum Arzt gehen

3. I want to go to the doctor's   c. Ich bin krank

4. doctor   d. der Arzt

5. I am ill   e. die Apotheke

7   Write these phrases out in German.

a)   I have stomach ache   d)   My leg hurts

b)   My nose hurts   e)   My back hurts

c)   I have earache   f)   I have a headache

Summary Questions

Look back through the section to help yourself answer the questions until you're sure you've got them all right. Then try the questions again without looking back. You can't say you know the stuff unless you can answer the whole lot without looking or peeping.

1) How do you ask a friend what their name is in German?

2) Write this conversation out in German:
"When's your birthday?"   "It's on the fifth of March."

3) Describe yourself in German. Mention your height, the colour of your eyes and the colour of your hair.

4) Which one of these sentences means "I'm lazy"?
a) Ich bin fleißig.   b) Ich bin faul.

5) Write down the names of everyone in your family, then write down the German phrases for what relation they are to you.

6) Say you've got one brother. Say he's called Finbar and he's ninety-five years old.

7) Write this sentence out in German:
"I've got a horse, a bird, a tortoise and a hamster."

8) Write "My horse is nasty," in German.

9) Write three headings — der, die and das. Write each of these words under the right heading:

Schrank	Stuhl	Garten	Sofa
Küche	Schlafzimmer	Badezimmer	Esszimmer
Bett	Kleiderschrank	Tisch	Wohnzimmer

10) Now write down what all the words from question 9) mean.

11) Answer this question in German: Was für Möbel gibt es in deinem Wohnzimmer?

12) Write these out in German:

a) eastern England   c) western Wales

b) southern Scotland   d) northern Northern Ireland

13) Say "I like living here because it's quiet." (Now say it like you mean it.)

14) Put these sentences about daily routine into a sensible order,
then translate them into English:

Ich wasche mich.   Ich gehe ins Bett.   Ich wache auf.

Ich esse Abendessen.   Ich esse Frühstück.   Ich gehe zur Schule.

Ich ziehe mich an.   Ich gehe nach Hause.   Ich putze mir die Zahne.

15) Write down "I tidy my room." and "I don't do anything."in German.

16) What do "Ich gehe einkaufen." and "Ich spüle." mean in English?

17) Write this out in German: I'm ill. My head hurts. I want to go to the hospital.

18) What do these three words mean? die Salbe   das Rezept   die Schmerztablette

School Subjects

You might not want to talk about school, but you need to be able to say which subjects you do.

School subjects — die Schulfächer

Learn all these subjects so you can say what you do. Tackle them one group at a time.

SCIENCE

science: (die) Naturwissenschaft
physics: (die) Physik
chemistry: (die) Chemie
biology: (die) Biologie

LANGUAGES

English: (das) Englisch
German: (das) Deutsch
French: (das) Französisch
Spanish: (das) Spanisch

PHYSICAL EDUCATION

PE: (der) Sport

HUMANITIES

history: (die) Geschichte
geography: (die) Erdkunde / (die) Geografie
religious studies: (die) Reli(gion)

ART AND MUSIC

art: (die) Kunst
music: (die) Musik

NUMBERS AND STUFF

maths: (die) Mathe(matik)
ICT: (die) Informatik

Say what you do

This is easy. It's just "ich lerne" + subject:

Ich lerne Deutsch.   = I study German.

This page is an education

You need to learn the words for all 16 subjects, even the ones you don't do. If you want to talk about any subjects that aren't on this page, have a look in a dictionary. Then learn them.

School Subjects

Now you can say which subjects you do, it's good to be able to say whether or not you like them.

My favourite subject — mein Lieblingsfach

Raise your German level a ton by giving opinions about your subjects.

You can put "Lieblings" in front of pretty much any "thing" to say it's your favourite. E.g. "Farbe" = "colour", "Lieblingsfarbe" = favourite colour."

SUBJECT + "ist mein Lieblingsfach"

Musik *ist mein Lieblingsfach.* = Music is my favourite subject.

You can replace the words in the green boxes with any of the subjects on page 35.

Ich mag **Geschichte**. = I like history.

Ich hasse **Geschichte**. = I hate history.

For more on opinions see p.99.

Give a reason for your choice

Ich mag **Geschichte**, *weil* **sie** **einfach** *ist.* = I like history because it is easy.

Remember, it's "er" for "der" words, "sie" for "die" words, "es" for "das" words (see p.109).

interesting:	interessant
easy:	einfach
useful:	nützlich

Ich hasse **Geschichte**, *weil* **sie** **langweilig** *ist.* = I hate history because it is boring.

boring:	langweilig
difficult:	schwierig
pointless:	nutzlos

It's probably best not to say you hate German

It doesn't matter what subjects you say you like or don't like, but it's great if you can add a reason. Learn the reasons above and practise writing opinions for all your different subjects.

School Routine

This page is all about what happens during your school day. You might know some of it already.

The school day — der Schultag

Go through these phrases, and write out your own version of each one so it matches your day.

Ich fahre mit dem Auto zur Schule.　= I go by car to school.

bus: Bus
bike: Fahrrad

For more on transport, see pages 77-78.

Ich gehe zu Fuß zur Schule.　= I go to school on foot.

For more on home routine, see p.26.

Ich stehe um acht Uhr auf.　= I get up at 8:00.

For more on times, see p.2.

Die Schule fängt um neun Uhr an.　= School begins at 9:00.

Die Schule ist um vier Uhr aus.　= School ends at 4:00.

Jede Stunde dauert vierzig Minuten.　= Each lesson lasts forty minutes.

Wir haben acht Stunden pro Tag.　= We have eight lessons per day.

For more on numbers, see p.1.

Wir machen eine Stunde Hausaufgaben pro Tag.

two hours: zwei Stunden

= We do one hour of homework every day.

School days — the happiest days of your life, or so they say

It's all good practice of numbers and times, which you can use all over the place. Watch out for the spellings — don't mix up 'an' with 'aus'. Even the tiny words have to be right.

Classroom Stuff

If you ever lose your pen, this vocab could be very useful. At least you'll know what to ask for.

In the classroom — **im Klassenzimmer**

When you're in German class, <u>use</u> the German words for the <u>classroom objects</u>.
Even if you just say "Where's my Kuli?" it'll help lodge the German words in your head.

book:
das Buch

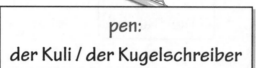

pen:
der Kuli / der Kugelschreiber

ruler:
das Lineal

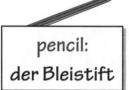

pencil:
der Bleistift

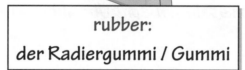

rubber:
der Radiergummi / Gummi

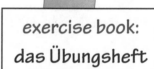

exercise book:
das Übungsheft

pupil:
der Schüler (lad)
die Schülerin (lass)

teacher:
der Lehrer (man)
die Lehrerin (woman)

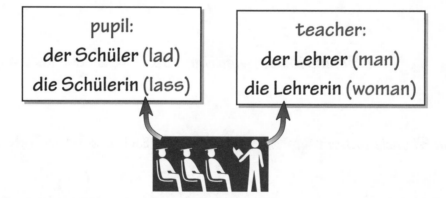

More school words

> *uniform:* die Uniform
> *lesson:* die Stunde
> *timetable:* der Stundenplan

Remember there are two words for teacher

Your female teacher may not be happy to be called a man. Also remember "Buch" is for proper printed books, and "Übungsheft" is for exercise books you write in. Very different.

Classroom Stuff

If your teacher's anything like mine was, they'll <u>talk to you in German</u>. Learn this page and if they're shouting "Seid ruhig!" you'll know what to do. Or you'll know what they want you to do.

Sit down! — Setzt euch!

Learn these phrases and you could avoid a lot of trouble.

Steht auf! = Stand up!

Hört zu! = Listen!

Setzt euch! = Sit down!

Seid ruhig! = Be quiet!

Use these phrases if you get a bit stuck

Was bedeutet das? = What does that mean?

Wie sagt man das auf Deutsch? = How do you say that in German?

Wie sagt man das auf Englisch? = How do you say that in English?

True or False?

richtig = true   **falsch** = false

Some very useful vocab to know

Once you've learnt these phrases, if you don't understand what someone is saying to you in German, you'll be able to ask them to say it in English. Great. Now get learning them.

Practice Questions

Track 7   Listening Questions

Mark is talking to his friends about the school subjects they like and dislike.
What are his friends' opinions of the following subjects?
Write 'positive', 'negative' or 'no information' for each one.

1   Maria   a) ICT   b) French   c) Music

2   Gregor   a) Geography   b) History   c) Art

3   Kristina   a) Maths   b) English   c) Science

4   Here are some school subjects in English. Write down what they are in German.

   a) ICT   d) music   g) sport

   b) chemistry   e) biology   h) French

   c) science   f) religious studies i) Spanish

5   Copy and complete these sentences, using the words from the box.

   a) Ich fahre mit dem .... zur Schule.

   b) Wir haben neun .... pro Tag.

   c) Die Schule .... um acht Uhr an.

   d) Ich gehe zu .... zur Schule.

   e) Jede Stunde dauert vierzig ....

   f) Ich .... um acht Uhr auf.

   | Stunden |
   | Minuten |
   | Fahrrad |
   | fängt |
   | Fuß |
   | stehe |

6   All these words are some kind of "classroom stuff".
     Write down what they are in English.

   a) der Stundenplan   c) der Gummi   e) das Übungsheft

   b) der Kuli   d) das Lineal   f) das Buch

7   Write these out in German:

   a) How do you say that in German?   d) What does that mean?

   b) Stand up!   e) Listen!

   c) true   f) teacher (woman)

Jobs

There are different words for job titles depending on whether it's a man or a woman doing the job. The ♂ words are for men, the ♀ ones are for women.

Here are the jobs — die Berufe

('der Beruf' = job)

Words ending with 'in' for women:

mechanic:
♂ Mechaniker
♀ Mechanikerin

builder:
♂ Bauarbeiter
♀ Bauarbeiterin

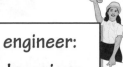

engineer:
♂ Ingenieur
♀ Ingenieurin

teacher:
♂ Lehrer
♀ Lehrerin

doctor:
♂ Arzt
♀ Ärztin

policeman/woman:
♂ Polizist
♀ Polizistin

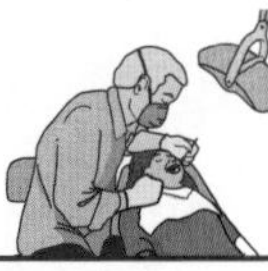

dentist:
♂ Zahnarzt
♀ Zahnärztin

salesperson:
♂ Verkäufer
♀ Verkäuferin

secretary:
♂ Sekretär
♀ Sekretärin

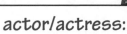

actor/actress:
♂ Schauspieler
♀ Schauspielerin

Words with different endings for men and women:

nurse:
♂ Krankenpfleger
♀ Krankenschwester

office worker:
♂ Büroangestellter
♀ Büroangestellte

hairdresser:
♂ Friseur
♀ Friseuse

Talking About Jobs

In the <u>old days</u>, you'd finish school and go to work up a <u>chimney</u>. Nowadays you have a few more options. <u>Learn</u> this German, and if you don't know what you want to do, just <u>pretend</u>.

Tell them what you **want to study**

Use this sentence for what you'd like <u>to study</u> (for GCSEs or A-levels):

"Ich möchte" + SUBJECT + "lernen"

Ich möchte Biologie lernen,...   = I would like to study biology...

See p.35 for more subjects.

Give a short reason <u>why</u>:

...weil ich Arzt werden möchte.   = ...because <u>I would like to be a doctor</u>.

it's easy: es einfach ist.
it's fun: es lustig ist.
it's interesting: es interessant ist.

Tell them what job you want

Talk about <u>jobs</u> like this:

"Ich möchte" + JOB + "werden"

Ich möchte Arzt werden,...   = I would like to become a doctor...

See p.41 for more jobs.

You can use any of the reasons from <u>above</u>, or this one:

...weil sie viel Geld verdienen.   = ...because they earn a lot of money.

Start thinking about the future now

For about the next five years, adults will be endlessly asking what you want to do with your life. German teachers are no different, so for minimum hassle get this stuff learned.

Talking About Jobs

This page is about how to say what job you have at the moment and what your parents do.

Say what **you do** and **other people do**

Work out and practise saying what <u>you do</u> (if you have a job), and what <u>your parents do</u>.
For <u>other</u> people, swap 'mein Vater' with e.g. 'mein Bruder' or 'meine Freundin Liz' (see p.16).

Ich bin Polizist.   = I am a policeman.

Meine Mutter ist Polizistin.   = My mother is a policewoman.

Mein Vater ist Polizist.   = My father is a policeman.

**Remember: Don't put 'ein' or 'eine'.
Just put 'bin' or 'ist' and the job.**

If you've got a <u>part-time job</u>, say what it is, or <u>where</u> you work:

Ich habe einen Teilzeitjob.   = I have a part-time job.

Ich arbeite bei Kwik Save.   = I work at Kwik Save.

Ich trage Zeitungen aus.   = I deliver newspapers.

Your job is to learn all of this

Feel free to make up different jobs for your friends and family — it may not be true, but you'll learn lots more German. I'm not sure anyone will believe that you are a dentist though.

Practice Questions

Listening Questions

Listen to these students talking about their future plans,
then answer the following questions.

1 a) Which subject does Stefan want to study?

   b) Who in Stefan's family is an engineer?

2 a) What does Lea want to study as well as Spanish?

   b) What two jobs does she say she might do?

3 a) Why does Mario like science?

   b) What two jobs does he say he might do?

4 Here you have a list of jobs in German. Copy out the table and write the jobs
in each column, depending on whether they're words for MEN or for WOMEN.
One has been done for you.

Büroangestellter   Krankenpfleger

Bauarbeiterin   Arzt

Krankenschwester   Zahnarzt

Schauspieler   Polizistin

~~Friseur~~   Ingenieurin

Mechanikerin   Lehrerin

Male	Female
Friseur	

5 Match the German sentences on the left to the English sentences on the right.

1. Ich bin Arzt

2. Mein Vater ist Mechaniker

3. Meine Mutter ist Verkäuferin

4. Mein Freund George ist Ingenieur

5. Ich arbeite bei Kwik Save

6. Ich habe einen Teilzeitjob

a. My friend George is an engineer

b. My father is a mechanic

c. I am a doctor

d. My mother is a salesperson

e. I have a part-time job

f. I work in Kwik Save

Summary Questions

You've looked out the window for a bit. You've had a little think about what you're going to do at the weekend. But still these darned questions are staring up at you. They're not going to go away. Answer all the questions — look back through the section for help at first, but aim to be able to answer every single one without looking back.

1) Write a German sentence starting "Ich lerne..." for every subject you do.

2) Write "Ich mag..." and "Ich hasse..." sentences for each of the subjects you wrote down for question 1.

3) Write a sentence using each of these words for three of the subjects from Q1:
   a) nutzlos   b)   langweilig   c) schwierig

4) What time do you normally get up? Answer in German.

5) What time does school end? Answer in German.

6) How long is each of your lessons? Answer in German.

7) How much homework do you have to do each day? Answer in German.

8) What kind of book is "das Buch"? What kind of book is "das Übungsheft"?

9) Write three headings — "der", "die" and "das",
   then copy these words out under the right headings.

Lehrer	Schülerin	Stundenplan	Kuli
Buch	Lehrerin	Übungsheft	Bleistift	Uniform
Lineal	Schüler	Gummi	Stunde

10) Write the English meaning next to each of the words from Q9.

11) If somebody says "Setzt euch!" what do they want you to do?

12) What could you say in German to find out what a German word means?
    Write down two ways of saying it.

13) Write down what each of these words means.

| Büroangestellte | Bauarbeiter | Lehrer | Verkäufer | Schauspielerin |
| Ingenieur | Sekretär | Polizistin | Ärztin | Zahnärztin |

14) Write in German:
    "I want to study history because it's interesting. I want to be an actor because it's fun."

15) Write two more sets of sentences like the ones in Q14. Write one about what you really want to do and one about the worst subject and job you can possibly imagine. Use a dictionary if you can't find the vocab.

16) What does "Meine Mutter ist Ärztin" mean in English?

17) Write down sentences to say what jobs everyone in your family does.

Directions

If you go to Germany and want to find out where something is, this page will be very useful.
You'll even be able to ask how far away things are — so you'll know if you need to get a bus.

Where is...? — Wo ist...?

You need to learn both these phrases for "Where's the...?" so you can understand and use them.
Swap "das Kino" for any place you like (see pages 48 and 49 for other places).

Wo ist das Kino, bitte?   = Where is the cinema, please?

Gibt es hier in der Nähe ein Kino?   = Is there a cinema near here?

Distances — say if it's near or far

You'll need to find out how far it is to where you want to go.

Wie weit ist es von hier?   = How far is it from here?

Es ist weit von hier.   = It's far from here.

Es ist in der Nähe von hier.   = It's near here.

Es ist zwei Kilometer von hier.   = It's two kilometres from here.

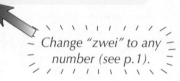

*Change "zwei" to any
number (see p.1).*

Where am I?

Teachers are always asking about this stuff, so the sooner you learn it the better. It's pretty
useful too if you're really hungry and want to find out where the nearest restaurant is.

Directions

One thing you <u>always</u> have to do in German lessons is use a dodgy map to give directions to the person sitting next to you. Even if you never go to Germany, you need to <u>learn</u> this stuff.

Giving directions

go left:

gehen Sie links

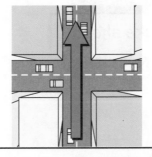

go straight on:

gehen Sie geradeaus

go right:

gehen Sie rechts

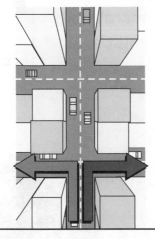

take the first street
on the left / right:

nehmen Sie die erste
Straße links / rechts

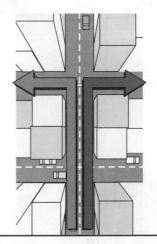

take the second street
on the left / right:

nehmen Sie die zweite
Straße links / rechts

These are useful phrases — especially if you're lost

If you're lost in Berlin and ask someone the way, you'll still be lost if you don't understand the directions they give you. Cover up the German and see if you can remember each phrase.

Shops

And now you get to learn the words for lots of different shops. Luckily there are only ten...

The shops — **die Geschäfte**   *("DAS GESCHÄFT" = SHOP)*

bakery:
die Bäckerei

cake shop:
die Konditorei

grocer's:
der Lebensmittelladen

butcher's:
die Metzgerei

pharmacist's:
die Apotheke

general chemist's:
die Drogerie

market:
der Markt

sweet shop:
das Süßwarengeschäft

supermarket:
der Supermarkt

bookshop:
die Buchhandlung

No time for shopping, but at least you get to learn about shops

Just ten bits of shop vocab to learn, but you need to make sure you know each one extra well.
That means spellings 100% right, from memory. Don't forget the "der", "die" or "das".

Places in Town

Places to go, things to see. Some of these are easy — they're exactly the <u>same</u> as the English. Look out for "das Theat<u>er</u>" though — the 'r' and the 'e' have been sneakily swapped around.

17 Places to **Learn**

museum:
das Museum

leisure centre:
das Freizeitzentrum

town hall:
das Rathaus

library:
die Bibliothek

bank:
die Bank

park:
der Park

cinema:
das Kino

train station:
der Bahnhof

swimming pool:
das Schwimmbad

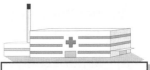

hospital:
das Krankenhaus

theatre:
das Theater

town centre:
die Stadtmitte

post office:
die Post

castle:
das Schloss

hotel:
das Hotel

tourist information:
das Verkehrsamt

church:
die Kirche

Practice Questions

Track 9   Listening Question

1   Birgit works in the tourist information office (ⓘ on the map below).
Listen to her giving directions to three customers (a-c).
For each one, write down the number on the map that Birgit directs them to.

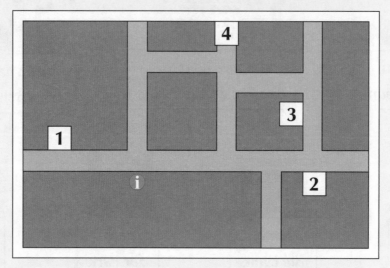

2   Answer these questions by choosing the right German shop from the box.
You can only use each shop once.

a)   Where can you buy a book?

b)   Where's your best bet for buying some bread?

c)   Where could you buy some headache tablets?

d)   Where can you buy a steak for your dog?

e)   Where's the best place to buy a birthday cake?

die Metzgerei
die Bäckerei
die Apotheke
die Konditorei
die Buchhandlung

3   Here are two lists of place names. Match the German words on the left to
the English words on the right.

1. das Kino   a. hospital
2. das Verkehrsamt   b. swimming pool
3. die Bibliothek   c. train station
4. das Schloss   d. library
5. der Bahnhof   e. town centre
6. das Krankenhaus   f. tourist office
7. die Stadtmitte   g. cinema
8. das Schwimmbad   h. castle

Fruit and Vegetables

On the plus side there are <u>no phrases</u> to learn on this page. On the down side it's all vocab.

Fruit — **das Obst**

apple:
der Apfel

pear:
die Birne

orange:
die Orange

lemon:
die Zitrone

peach:
der Pfirsich

strawberry:
die Erdbeere

banana:
die Banane

Vegetables — **das Gemüse**

tomato:
die Tomate

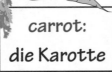

carrot:
die Karotte

cabbage:
der Kohl

lettuce:
der Kopfsalat

cauliflower:
der Blumenkohl

onion:
die Zwiebel

peas:
die Erbsen

mushroom:
der Pilz

potato:
die Kartoffel

"Blumenkohl" means "flower cabbage"

Don't let this page scare you with all its healthiness — you need to learn this vocab.
Try copying it all out, and then copy it again. Keep going until you can do it without looking.

Meat and Other Foods

Now it's time to learn some proper food vocab. This page is all about <u>meat</u> and <u>stodge</u>.

Meat — das Fleisch

pork:
das Schweinefleisch

lamb:
das Lammfleisch

beef:
das Rindfleisch

chicken:
das Hähnchen

steak:
das Steak

ham:
der Schinken

sausage:
die Wurst

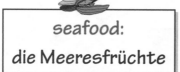

seafood:
die Meeresfrüchte

fish:
der Fisch

Other stuff — mainly stodge

bread:
das Brot

pasta:
die Nudeln

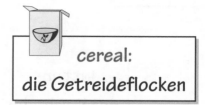

cereal:
die Getreideflocken

rice:
der Reis

chips:
die Pommes frites

crisps:
die Kartoffelchips

It's not all sausages you know

I mean, there are lots of sausages in Germany, never mind Austria and Switzerland. But there are other things too, like ham, and salami, and roast pork, and pig knuckles. Mmmm.

Sweet Things and Dairy

Right, time for some serious concentration — some of the most important vocab in this book is <u>right here</u> on this page. Ahem, cake, ahem.

Sweet things — **die Süßigkeiten**

Learn these words about delicious, sweet, <u>sugary</u> things.

cake:
der Kuchen

chocolate:
die Schokolade

biscuits:
die Kekse

jam:
die Marmelade

sugar:
der Zucker

ice cream:
das Eis

Dairy products

milk:
die Milch

yoghurt:
der Joghurt

cheese:
der Käse

butter:
die Butter

cream:
die Sahne

egg:
das Ei

That should be most of the food you'll need

You'll always get a good feed in Germany. Unless you don't know any food vocab. Learn it all and make sure you know what's "der", "die" and "das". Copying things out helps loads.

Drinks

If you're tired of food vocab, don't worry — you can learn some drinks vocab instead.

Drinks — **die Getränke**

Here are some <u>cold drinks</u> to get you started...

"Saft" means "juice" — you can add it to the end of any fruit from p.51 to make that type of fruit juice.

cola:

die Cola

mineral water:

das Mineralwasser

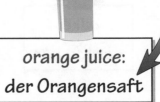

orange juice:

der Orangensaft

beer:

das Bier

red wine:

der Rotwein

white wine:

der Weißwein

Hot drinks and soup

And now for the hot drinks...

tea:

der Tee

coffee:

der Kaffee

hot chocolate:

die heiße Schokolade

soup:

die Suppe

It must be time for a tea break now

These are just a few drinks that you should learn. If your favourite drink isn't here, see if you can find it in the dictionary. Then learn that one too. It's all useful stuff.

Talking About Food

If you love food, you're in luck — here's a whole page of <u>talking about food</u>.

I like... — Ich mag...

These "like" / "don't like" phrases come up <u>all over the place</u>, so get them <u>learned</u>.

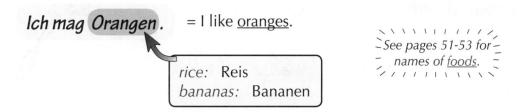

Ich mag **Orangen**.   = I like <u>oranges</u>.

> rice: Reis
> bananas: Bananen

See pages 51-53 for names of <u>foods</u>.

Ich mag **Orangen** nicht.   = I don't like <u>oranges</u>.

See p.99 for more on <u>opinions</u>.

> peas: Erbsen
> cream: Sahne

I'm hungry — Ich habe Hunger...

The normal German phrase for "I'm hungry" is "Ich habe Hunger" — literally, "I <u>have</u> hunger."

Hast du Hunger?

= Are you hungry?

Hast du Durst?

= Are you thirsty?

Ja, ich habe Hunger.

= Yes, I am hungry.

Ja, ich habe Durst.

= Yes, I am thirsty.

Nein, ich habe keinen Hunger.

= No, I am not hungry.

Nein, ich habe keinen Durst.

= No, I am not thirsty.

I like rice and peas

Practise writing which foods you like and don't like. All you need to do is put "Ich mag" and then a type of food. Easy. If you decide you don't like it, just add on "nicht" after the food.

Talking About Food

You need to be able to say <u>what you eat</u> and <u>what time</u> you have your meals.
It's truly fascinating stuff...

Say what you eat

Ich esse Wurst . = I eat <u>sausage</u>.

Ich trinke Wasser . = I drink <u>water</u>.

See pages 51-54 for more food and drink words.

Say when you eat

breakfast:
das Frühstück

lunch:
das Mittagessen

evening meal:
das Abendessen

Das Frühstück ist um acht Uhr . = Breakfast is at <u>8 o'clock</u>.

See p.2 for clock times.

Das Mittagessen ist um halb eins . = Lunch is at <u>half past twelve</u>.

Das Abendessen ist um sieben Uhr . = The evening meal is at <u>7 o'clock</u>.

These are some very useful phases

This is where knowing your times comes in handy — you wouldn't want to miss out on dinner.
Practise saying what time you eat breakfast, lunch and dinner. Then practise again.

In a Restaurant

Restaurants are a <u>key topic</u> for <u>KS3 German</u>, and dead useful for holidays.

General vocab

"das Restaurant" should be pretty easy to remember...

restaurant:

das Restaurant

waiter:

der Kellner

waitress:

die Kellnerin

At the table

menu:

die Speisekarte

drink:

das Getränk

starter:

die Vorspeise

main course:

das Hauptgericht

dessert:

der Nachtisch

Make sure you've learnt all these words

The words for "starter", "main course" and "dessert" are handy for knowing which part of the menu you're looking at. They're also useful for restaurant role-plays and other fun things.

In a Restaurant

Now it's time to put the vocabulary <u>into practice</u> and go to a restaurant.

Restaurant **Conversations**

Get yourself a table, order what you want to eat and drink, and pay at the end:

(1) Get yourself a <u>table</u>:

Einen Tisch für zwei Personen, bitte. = A table for <u>two</u>, please.

Stick any number from p.1 here. One person is "eine Person".

(2) The waiter/waitress asks <u>what you want</u>:

Was möchten Sie? = What would you like?

Ich hätte gern Fisch. = I would like <u>fish</u>.

There are more food and drink words on p.51-54.

Etwas zu trinken? = Anything to drink?

Ich nehme eine Cola. = I'll have a <u>cola</u>.

(3) At the end of the meal, <u>say you'd like to pay</u>:

Zahlen, bitte. = I'd like to pay, please.

Practise this as a role-play with a friend

"Ich hätte gern..." is a great phrase to learn — you can use it whenever and wherever you want something, and sound dead polite too, e.g. "Ich hätte gern ein Auto" = I would like a car.

Practice Questions

Track 10   <u>Listening Question</u>

1   Listen to these three customers (a-c) placing their orders in a restaurant.
    Write down what each person orders from this list.

carrot soup	sausage and chips	cola
mushroom soup	seafood pasta	red wine
onion soup	chicken and chips	white wine
	pork with potatoes	mineral water
	fish with potatoes	

2   Here are some items of food in English. Write down what they are in German.

a)   lamb   d)   beef

b)   seafood   e)   ham

c)   pork   f)   chicken

3   Write these shopping lists out in English.

```
○○○○○○○○○○○○○○○
      SUPERMARKT
      eine Wurst
       Fisch
       Steak
       Pilze
    ein Blumenkohl
    vier Kartoffeln
      ein Kohl
    ein Kopfsalat
    fünf Karotten
```

```
○○○○○○○○○○○○○○○○○
    LEBENSMITTELLADEN
      zwei Zitronen
       eine Birne
       ein Apfel
      eine Zwiebel
        Erbsen
     drei Pfirsiche
      eine Banane
      vier Orangen
```

Practice Questions

4   Read through this restaurant drinks list and answer the questions below.

Apfelsaft	Cola	Bier	Weißwein	Kaffee
Orangensaft	Mineralwasser	Rotwein	heiße Schokolade	Tee

a)   Using the drinks list above, write the names of these drinks in German.

1. coffee

2. mineral water

3. orange juice

4. hot chocolate

5. cola

b)   Copy out the five other words from the drinks list and write what they mean in English.

5   How would you say these things in German?

a)   Are you thirsty?

b)   I don't like chocolate.

c)   I'm hungry.

d)   I don't like jam.

e)   I'm not thirsty.

f)   I like milk.

6   Read about Lisa's eating habits, then answer the questions in English.

Das Frühstück ist um sieben Uhr.
Ich esse Getreideflocken und trinke
Kaffee.

Das Mittagessen ist um ein Uhr.
Ich esse Schweinefleisch und Reis.
Ich trinke Cola.

Das Abendessen ist um acht Uhr.
Ich esse Hähnchen und Nudeln.
Ich trinke Weißwein.

Lisa

a)   What time does Lisa eat breakfast?

b)   What does Lisa have for breakfast?

c)   What does Lisa eat and drink at lunchtime?

d)   What time does Lisa eat lunch?

e)   What does Lisa eat and drink for dinner?

Clothes

Learn your clothing — die Kleidung

There's a lot to learn here. <u>Break it down</u> into <u>chunks</u> of 4 items, and learn 'em a chunk at a time.

shirt: das Hemd

blouse: die Bluse

T-shirt: das T-Shirt

jumper: der Pullover

jacket: die Jacke

dress: das Kleid

skirt: der Rock

coat: der Mantel

raincoat: der Regenmantel

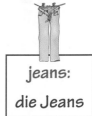
jeans: die Jeans

tie: die Krawatte

hat: der Hut

trousers: die Hose

glasses: die Brille

Although 'trousers' and 'glasses' are plural in English, in German they are both singular feminine.

shoe / shoes: der Schuh / die Schuhe

glove / gloves: der Handschuh / die Handschuhe

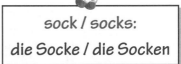
sock / socks: die Socke / die Socken

Say what you wear

"Ich trage" + "einen / eine / ein" + GARMENT

To say "he/she is wearing", it's "er/sie <u>trägt</u>".

Ich trage ein T-Shirt. ⬅ It's "<u>einen</u>" for "<u>der</u>" things, "<u>eine</u>" for "<u>die</u>" things, "<u>ein</u>" for "<u>das</u>" things. See p.113.

= I'm wearing a T-shirt.

Ich trage Handschuhe. ⬅ Socks, shoes and gloves are all <u>plurals</u>. You <u>don't</u> need to use "einen", "eine" or "ein" with these.

= I'm wearing gloves.

Colours and Materials

Colour words are useful for lots of things, but they're especially good for <u>describing</u> your <u>clothes</u>.

Learn these **colours**...

 black:
schwarz

 grey:
grau

 white:
weiß

 red:
rot

 yellow:
gelb

 green:
grün

 blue:
blau

 pink:
rosa

 orange:
orange

 brown:
braun

To say what colour something is, put the colour first.

E.g.   *der weiß<u>e</u> Rock*   = the white skirt

To be 100% correct you have to stick an ending on the colour word — see p.117.

...and these **materials**

 wool:
die Wolle

 cotton:
die Baumwolle

 leather:
das Leder

You can add a material to a garment to make one giant word.
(But drop the "<u>e</u>" from Woll<u>e</u> and Baumwoll<u>e</u>.)

E.g.   *ein Wollpullover*   = a woollen jumper

Describe your **school uniform**

*Ich trage eine graue Hose, einen Wollpullover,
eine schwarze Krawatte, und ein Baumwollhemd.*

= I wear grey trousers, a woollen jumper,
a black tie and a cotton shirt.

Asking for Things

How can you <u>shop</u> without <u>words</u>... and how can you <u>live</u> without <u>shopping</u>...

Asking for stuff — **ich möchte...**

Here are some phrases that come in useful when you're out shopping. Learn how to ask the shop assistant for what you want and then say whether you actually want to buy it.

Ich möchte einen Rock .

OR

Ich hätte gern einen Rock . = I would like <u>a skirt</u>.

Stick "bitte" on the end of these to make them more polite.

Ich nehme das. OR *Ich lasse es.*

= I'll take that one. = I'll leave it.

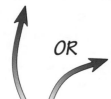

The shop assistant might ask if you want anything else...

Sonst noch etwas?

OR

Sonst noch einen Wunsch? = Anything else?

...in which case you could say something like...

Ja, bitte. OR *Nein, danke.*

= Yes, please. = No, thank you.

Practise using these phrases

There are a couple of different ways here for saying "I would like..." and "Anything else?".
Make sure you know each one so you can understand them. They're also good for showing off.

Prices

Unfortunately if you want to buy anything, you'll have to pay for it. Best to learn how then.

Asking how much things cost

Was kostet das?   = How much is that?

Das kostet zwei Euro.   = It costs <u>two</u> euros.

There are more numbers on p.1.

OR   **Zwei Euro.**   = <u>Two</u> euros.

German money — the **euro**

German money's easy — there are <u>100 cents</u> in a <u>euro</u>, like there are 100 pence in a pound.

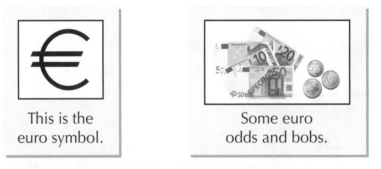

This is the euro symbol.

Some euro odds and bobs.

This is what you'd <u>see</u> on a German <u>price tag</u>.
They use a <u>comma</u>, not a decimal point:

€ 5,50

This is how you <u>say</u> the price on the price tag: *"fünf Euro fünfzig Cent"*

These phrases are actually useful in real life

Learn your numbers and you won't have any problems understanding prices. Just remember German prices have a comma instead of a decimal point. Strange, but you get used to it.

Practice Questions

Track 11   Listening Question

1   Beate is shopping for clothes.
Listen to the conversation, then answer these questions in English.

    a)   What does Beate ask for first?

    b)   Why does she not buy this item?

    c)   What does she ask for next?

    d)   What does it cost?

2   Write these sentences out in English. The first one has been done for you.

    a)   Ich trage einen blauen Pullover.   *I'm wearing a blue jumper.*

    b)   Frau Becker trägt einen rosa Regenmantel.

    c)   Tobias trägt eine grüne Hose.

    d)   Anna trägt einen weißen Rock.

    e)   Mein Vater trägt einen grauen Hut.

    f)   Er trägt eine rote Krawatte.

3   Describe what these people are wearing, in German.
Don't forget to mention the colours and materials.

    a)

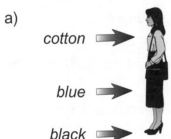

cotton

blue

black

    b)

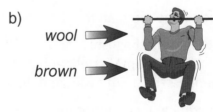

wool

brown

4   Write these phrases out in English. Choose from the English phrases in the box.

    a)   Sonst noch etwas?

    b)   Ich lasse es.

    c)   Was kostet das?

    d)   Ich nehme das.

    e)   Das kostet zehn Euro.

> It's 10 euros.
> I'll take that one.
> I'll leave it.
> How much is that?
> Anything else?

Summary Questions

And now some more questions to test what you know... They're not fun, but they are the only way to find out whether you really know your stuff. Do these questions till you can get all the answers right without looking back through the book (or over your mate's shoulder).

1) Ask where the museum is in German.

2) Translate this into English:
"Gehen Sie geradeaus. Nehmen Sie die zweite Straße links, und dann die erste Straße links."

3) Ask how far away the museum is and translate this answer:
"Es ist sechshundert Meter von hier."

4) Write down two German "der" names for shops, two "die" names, and one "das" one.

5) Sort these words out into three columns headed "der", "die" and "das":

   Bahnhof   Kirche   Theater   Bibliothek   Verkehrsamt   Rathaus
   Park   Hotel   Museum   Bank   Post   Freizeitzentrum

6) Now translate all the words from Q5) into English.

7) Write down the German names of six different types of meat.

8) Make a list, in German, of fruit and vegetables you like.

9) Make a list, in German, of fruit and vegetables you don't like.

10) Write down the German for: a) cheese b) cream c) cake d) biscuits e) egg

11) There's one mistake in each of these words for drinks.
Copy them out and correct the mistakes.

   die Supe   die Kola   der Weisswein   die Tee   der Koffee   der Orangensaft

12) Write down the German for "I eat meat. I drink orange juice."

13) Translate this into English:
Das Frühstück ist um Viertel nach acht. Das Mittagessen ist um dreizehn Uhr.
Das Abendessen ist um zwanzig Uhr.

14) Write down the German for menu, starter, main course and pudding, including the "der", "die" or "das".

15) How would you ask for a table for two in German?

16) What's this in English? "Was möchten Sie?", "Ich hätte gern Lammfleisch".

17) How do you ask for the bill in German?

18) Make a list of things you normally wear at the weekend (in German), including the colours and materials.

19) You want to buy a loaf of bread. The shopkeeper says "Das kostet drei Euro."
How much is it?

Sport

If you love sport, you're in luck. This is a whole page of sports and how to say you play them.

Talk about sport — der Sport

Make sure you learn all these sports, even the ones you don't play.

football:
der Fußball

tennis:
das Tennis

table tennis:
das Tischtennis

cricket:
das Kricket

rugby:
das Rugby

badminton:
der Federball

chess:
das Schach

How to say what you play

This is really simple. It's just:

"Ich spiele" + SPORT

Ich spiele Fußball.   = I play football.

Ich spiele Tennis.   *Ich spiele Schach.*

= I play tennis.   = I play chess.

Learning German — it's all fun and games

Try this for a good game: get two strips of paper to cover up the words for each sport. Then on the paper, write down the German. Keep doing it till you can get them all right from memory.

Musical Instruments

You might not actually play a musical instrument, but now's your chance to pretend you do.

Learn the instruments — die Instrumente
[das Instrument = instrument]

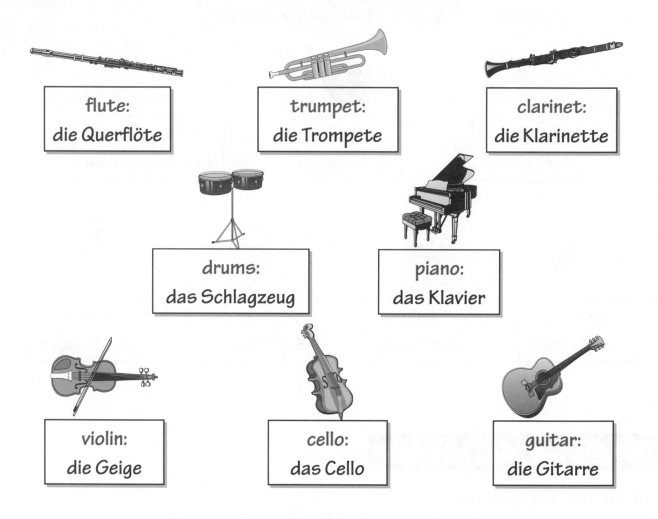

flute:
die Querflöte

trumpet:
die Trompete

clarinet:
die Klarinette

drums:
das Schlagzeug

piano:
das Klavier

violin:
die Geige

cello:
das Cello

guitar:
die Gitarre

How to say what you play

"Ich spiele" + INSTRUMENT

Ich spiele Gitarre   = I play the guitar.

Make sure you know all these instruments

Some of the German words for these instruments sound a bit like the English, so that should help you remember them. Watch out for the spellings though, as they can be a bit tricky.

Pastimes and Hobbies

Here are some more pastimes, but these are ones you <u>do</u> rather than play.

What do you do in your free time?

Was machst du in deiner Freizeit?

Ich gehe wandern.

= I go hiking.

Ich gehe schwimmen.

= I go swimming.

Ich gehe einkaufen.

= I go shopping.

Ich fahre Rad.

= I cycle.

Ich gehe kegeln.

= I go bowling.

Ich gehe Schlittschuh laufen .

= I go ice-skating.

I like to go shopping — Ich gehe gern einkaufen

You can add "<u>gern</u>" or "<u>nicht gern</u>" after the verb to say whether
you "<u>like</u>" or "<u>don't like</u>" doing any of the activities above.

EXAMPLES:

Ich gehe <u>gern</u> einkaufen.   = I <u>like</u> to go shopping.

Ich fahre <u>nicht gern</u> Rad.   = I <u>don't like</u> to cycle.

The verb is the "action word", e.g. "gehe" or "fahre". There's more on verbs on pages 123-124.

Six very important activities to learn

Even if you don't do any of these, you still need to know them. Practise saying that you do
each of them. Then practise writing them out. Then say that you do each of them. Then...

TV, Books and Radio

Put down your ice axe and pick up the <u>remote control</u>. This page is more relaxing.

I listen to the radio — Ich höre Radio

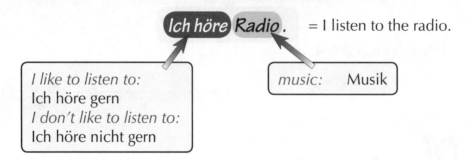

Ich höre Radio.   = I listen to the radio.

I like to listen to:
Ich höre gern
I don't like to listen to:
Ich höre nicht gern

music: Musik

I read books — Ich lese Bücher

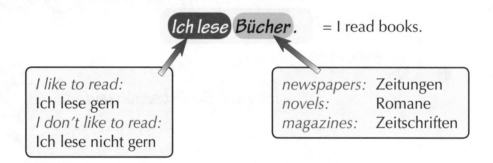

Ich lese Bücher.   = I read books.

I like to read:
Ich lese gern
I don't like to read:
Ich lese nicht gern

newspapers: Zeitungen
novels: Romane
magazines: Zeitschriften

I watch television — Ich sehe fern

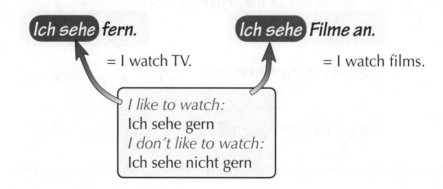

Ich sehe fern.
= I watch TV.

Ich sehe Filme an.
= I watch films.

I like to watch:
Ich sehe gern
I don't like to watch:
Ich sehe nicht gern

Add "gern" to say "like" and "nicht gern" to say "don't like"

Watch out for the word order though — Germans literally say "I watch like TV" instead of "I like to watch TV" and "I read don't like books" instead of "I don't like to read books". Very odd.

Likes and Dislikes

Now you get to learn more ways of saying whether you like or don't like different activities. You also get to say why you like them. I know, I spoil you rotten...

I like Tennis — Ich mag Tennis

You can swap "Tennis" for any of the sports from p.67.

Magst du Tennis? = Do you like tennis?

Ich mag Tennis
= I like tennis

Ich liebe Tennis
= I love tennis

..., weil es interessant ist.
= ...because it's interesting.

easy: einfach
fun: lustig

Ich mag Tennis nicht
= I don't like tennis

Ich hasse Tennis
= I hate tennis

..., weil es langweilig ist.
= ...because it's boring.

difficult: schwierig
tiring: ermüdend

It's "er" for "der" words, "sie" for "die" words, "es" for "das" words. See p.109.

I like this film — Ich mag diesen Film

Ich mag diesen Film.
= I like this film.

Ich mag diesen Film nicht.
= I don't like this film.

this music: diese Musik
this newspaper: diese Zeitung
this novel: diesen Roman
this magazine: diese Zeitschrift

I like learning German because it's fun

You need to be able to say your opinion to get the top levels. Write some sentences about the activities that you like and don't like, then see if you can add a reason to explain why.

Practice Questions

Track 12 Listening Questions

Listen to these people talking about their hobbies.
Say whether each of the following sentences is true or false.

1 a) Isabel likes hiking.

  b) She says she likes reading newspapers.

2 a) Joshua hates watching films on TV.

  b) His favourite sport is rugby.

3 a) Olivia loves shopping.

  b) Her favourite hobby is ice-skating.

4 The words in these sentences are in the wrong order.
  Write them in the correct order.

  a) spiele Kricket und Schach ich Trompete

  b) ich Klavier Geige und Federball spiele

  c) Fußball spiele Tennis und spiele ich Schlagzeug und ich

  d) Schach Tischtennis und Klarinette spiele ich

5 What do these sentences mean in English?

  a) Ich höre Musik.   c) Ich sehe Filme an.

  b) Ich lese Zeitschriften.   d) Ich lese Romane.

6 Write these opinions out in German. The first one has been done for you.

  a) ☺ + football   *Ich mag Fußball.*

  b) ☺☺ + badminton

  c) ☹ + chess

  d) ☹☹ + tennis

KEY
☺ = like
☺☺ = love
☹ = don't like
☹☹ = hate

7 Put these reasons into German. The first one has been done for you.

  a) because it is fantastic   *, weil es fantastisch ist.*

  b) because it is easy

  c) because it is boring

  d) because it is tiring

  e) because it is interesting

Places to Go

Some more vocab, but it's pretty useful — especially if you want to go on a date.

Places to Go

These are the main places you'd want to go. They're the places I'd want to go anyway.

home:

zu Hause

town centre:

die Stadtmitte

restaurant:

das Restaurant

cinema:

das Kino

theatre:

das Theater

leisure centre:

das Freizeitzentrum

swimming pool:

das Schwimmbad

Places to go, people to see

This vocab comes up all over the place, so you might as well learn it now. You can use it to ask people directions, ask people to meet up, tell people where you're going... It's great. Learn it.

Going Out and Making Arrangements

You need to learn this page so you can actually ask people to meet up. Otherwise you'll just have to shout "cinema" and hope they understand what you mean. Not ideal.

Do you want to...?

Use this phrase with one of the places on page 73.

"Hast du Lust" + "in den"/"in die"/"ins" + PLACE + "zu gehen"?

Hast du Lust ins Kino zu gehen?

= Do you want to go to the cinema?

*It's "in den" for "der" words,
"in die" for "die" words,
and "ins" for "das" words.*

"Zu Hause" is the odd one out. You don't put "ins zu Hause" —
you say "nach Hause".

Replying to invitations

"YES" PHRASES

Ja, gerne.

= Yes, I'd like to.

Ja, das wäre schön.

= Yes, I'd love to.

Ja, gute Idee.

= Yes, good idea.

"NO" PHRASES

Nein, danke.

= No, thank you.

Ich gehe nicht gern ins Kino.

= I don't like going to the cinema.

Ich habe kein Geld.

= I don't have any money.

Ich mache meine Hausaufgaben.

= I'm doing my homework.

No going out till you've learnt this page

You'll need to learn both the "yes" and "no" phrases because you can't be sure who's going to ask you out. So get learning them. Cover up the German and see if you can remember it.

Going Out and Making Arrangements

This page is all about arranging when and where to meet.

When shall we meet? — **Wann treffen wir uns?**

Be specific...   **Treffen wir uns *um zwanzig Uhr*.**   = Let's meet <u>at</u> <u>eight o'clock</u> (pm).

You can stick any <u>clock times</u> in here — see p.2.

at eleven o'clock (am): um elf Uhr
at two o'clock (pm): um vierzehn Uhr

Or be vague...   **Treffen wir uns *heute Abend*.**   = Let's meet <u>this evening</u>.

For other <u>days of the week</u>, see p.3.

tomorrow: morgen
tomorrow morning: morgen früh
on Thursday: am Donnerstag

Where shall we meet? — **Wo treffen wir uns?**

Treffen wir uns *in der Stadt*.   = Let's meet <u>in town</u>.

in the restaurant: im Restaurant
at my house: bei mir zu Hause

When you're meeting <u>in</u> a place say "im" for "der" and "das" words, and "in der" for "die" words.

There's a new word here — "<u>vor</u>", which means "in front of".

Treffen wir uns *vor dem Schwimmbad*.   = Let's meet <u>in front of the swimming pool</u>.

Here you need "dem" for "der" and "das" words, and "der" for "die" words. See p.114.

in front of the cinema: vor dem Kino
in front of the theatre: vor dem Theater

Practise planning to meet yourself

Think up a time and place and then see if you can suggest meeting yourself there — in German of course. Make sure you learn the questions too. It's classic role-play stuff.

Going Out and Making Arrangements

Once you've arranged to meet someone, you might need to buy some tickets.

Buying Tickets

If you want to go to the cinema or the theatre and you don't have a ticket, they won't let you in. Learn these few phrases to help you buy one.

Was kostet eine Karte, bitte? = How much does a ticket cost?

Eine Karte kostet zehn Euro. = A ticket costs ten euros.

There's more on German money on p.64.

Ich möchte eine Karte, bitte. = I would like a ticket, please.

| two tickets: | zwei Karten |
| three tickets: | drei Karten |

Putting it all together

You need to be able to put all the phrases to do with making arrangements together. Look back over the last few pages and see if you can put this conversation into German:

Person 1	Person 2
"Do you want to go to the leisure centre?"	"Yes, I'd love to."
"When shall we meet?"	"Let's meet at six o'clock in the evening."
"Where shall we meet?"	"Let's meet at my house."

Ich möchte zehn Karten, bitte.

You can use this phrase to ask for as many tickets as you like, but you'll probably just want one or two. Remember, "Karten" is the plural version — use it if you want more than one ticket.

Transport

This is all great stuff to use in Germany — it should help you get on the <u>tram</u> to the <u>zoo</u> and not the <u>train</u> to <u>Moscow</u> anyway. You can use it to talk about how you get around at home too.

Learn the names of these vehicles

car:
das Auto

bus:
der Bus

coach:
der Reisebus

bicycle:
das Fahrrad

motorbike:
das Motorrad

train:
der Zug

underground:
die U-Bahn

tram:
die Straßenbahn

ship:
das Schiff

aeroplane:
das Flugzeug

You need to know the words for all of these vehicles

It's dead easy this page — just ten bits of vocab to learn, and of course remembering which ones are "der", "die" and "das". Cover up the labels and see if you know them already.

Transport

Now you get to use your transport vocabulary to talk about how you travel around.

I go by... — Ich fahre mit...

This phrase comes up when you're talking about <u>going out</u>, <u>going to school</u> and <u>holidays</u>.

> **"Ich fahre mit dem/der" + VEHICLE**

Ich fahre mit dem Auto.   = I go by car.

You can use this phrase for all of the transport types from p.77, except planes (see below). Here are the <u>three other most common</u> ones:

Ich fahre mit dem Zug.   = I go by train.

Ich fahre mit dem Bus.   = I go by bus.

> It's <u>mit dem</u> for "der" and "das" words, and <u>mit der</u> for "die" words (see pages 114-115).

Ich fahre mit dem Fahrrad.   = I go by bike.

There are special phrases for <u>going on foot</u> and <u>going by aeroplane</u>:

Ich gehe zu Fuß.   = I go by foot.

Ich reise mit dem Flugzeug.   = I travel by plane.

OR   *Ich fliege.*   = I fly.

I go by spaceship

If you use a different method of transport, you'll have to look it up in a dictionary. Otherwise just remember you can use "ich fahre" for most types of transport, but not planes.

Transport

Germany has good trains that actually work, if you can imagine that.
There are quite a few phrases to learn here, but it's all essential stuff.

Train enquiries

Fährt ein Zug nach Berlin? = Is there <u>a train</u> going to Berlin?

Wann fährt der Zug nach Berlin?

If you're travelling by bus, change "<u>ein Zug</u>" to "<u>ein Bus</u>" and "<u>der Zug</u>" to "<u>der Bus</u>".

= When does <u>the train</u> for Berlin leave?

For more times, see p2.

Der Zug nach Berlin fährt um neun Uhr.

= The train for Berlin leaves at nine o'clock.

Von welchem Gleis fährt der Zug nach Berlin?

= Which platform does the train for Berlin leave from?

Der Zug nach Berlin fährt von Gleis drei.

= The train for Berlin leaves from platform three.

Buying tickets

Was für eine Fahrkarte brauchen Sie?

= What kind of ticket do you need?

second class: zweite Klasse

Eine einfache Fahrkarte nach Berlin, erste Klasse, bitte.

= <u>A single ticket</u> to Berlin, <u>1st class</u>, please.

a return ticket: eine Rückfahrkarte

You can use these phrases for buses as well as trains

Make sure you've got it sussed — test yourself by rewriting this in German (answer on p.150):
"Is there a train to München? I would like a return, first class. When does the train leave?"

Practice Questions

<u>Listening Questions</u>

1   Listen to these conversations (a-d).
    For each one, choose the reason for not going out from this list.

    1   is ill

    2   has missed the last train

    3   has got homework to do

    4   is travelling to Spain

    5   has no money

    6   doesn't like going there

Track 14

2   Listen to this conversation between a customer and a station employee at the
    ticket office. Answer these questions in English.

    a)   What sort of ticket does the customer want?

    b)   How much does it cost?

    c)   When is the next train leaving?

    d)   Which platform is it leaving from?

3   Write down **in German** where you'd do each of these things.
    All the words you need are in the box. The first one has been done for you.

    a)   See all the sights and do a bit of shopping

         die Stadtmitte

    b)   Go for a workout or a game of squash

    c)   Watch a film

    d)   Improve your doggy paddle

    e)   Go for dinner

    f)   See a play

    g)   Watch telly and have a nice cup of tea

das Restaurant
zu Hause
das Schwimmbad
die Stadtmitte
das Theater
das Freizeitzentrum
das Kino

Practice Questions

4 Write out the missing bits of this conversation about arranging to go to the cinema, **in German**.

> You: *[Do you want to go to the cinema?]*
>
> Dieter: Ja, das wäre schön. Wann treffen wir uns?
>
> You: *[Let's meet at seven o'clock (pm).]*
>
> Sophie: Ja, gerne. Und wo?
>
> You: *[Let's meet in front of the tourist office.]*   *Hint: tourist office = das Verkehrsamt*

5 Translate the missing bits of this conversation into German.

> You: *[How much does a ticket cost, please?]*
>
> Verkäuferin: Eine Karte kostet fünf Euro.
>
> You: *[I would like four tickets, please.]*
>
> Verkäuferin: Zwanzig Euro.
>
> You: *[Thank you.]*

6 Write these vehicles' names out in English.

> a) der Reisebus   d) die Straßenbahn
>
> b) die U-Bahn   e) der Zug
>
> c) das Schiff   f) der Bus

7 Here are Lisa's travel plans for the next week.
For each day, write down **where** she's going, and **how**.

> a) *Montag* Ich fahre mit dem Auto nach Mainz.
>
> b) *Dienstag* Ich gehe zu Fuß nach Bonn.
>
> c) *Mittwoch* Ich fahre mit dem Fahrrad zur Schule.
>
> d) *Donnerstag* Ich fahre mit dem Reisebus nach Italien.
>
> e) *Freitag* Ich reise mit dem Flugzeug nach Frankreich.

Summary Questions

So now you're all ready to head off to the chess clubs of Köln, and the railway stations of Regensburg. Before you get on the internet to book your tickets, make sure you know the stuff by doing the questions. All the questions. Till you get them all right without trying.

1) Write down the German for each of these:
   a) rugby b) table tennis c) cricket d) football e) badminton f) tennis
   Don't forget the "der", "die" and "das" — it's too easy otherwise.

2) What are these called in English?
   a) die Gitarre b) das Klavier c) die Querflöte d) das Schlagzeug e) die Geige

3) Write out three German sentences starting "Ich spiele" about sports or instruments.

4) How do you say these in German?
   a) I cycle. b) I go bowling. c) I go shopping. d) I go hiking. e) I go ice-skating.

5) Write a German sentence using "Ich ... gern ... " or "Ich ... nicht gern ... "
   about each of these:
   a) cricket   b) listening to the radio   c) watching TV
   d) going shopping   e) going ice-skating

6) What do these questions mean in English?
   a) Hast du Lust ins Theater zu gehen?
   b) Hast du Lust ins Freizeitzentrum zu gehen?

7) What's wrong with this question?
   "Hast du Lust ins Hause zu gehen?"

8) Your German exchange partner's good-looking cousin asks whether you want
   to go to the town centre. Write down three different ways of saying 'yes'.

9) Your German exchange partner's creepy-looking cousin asks whether you want
   to go to a restaurant. You definitely don't want to go. Say no politely, and
   make an excuse.

10) The gorgeous cousin asks you a question. What does it mean?
    "Um wie viel Uhr treffen wir uns?"

11) Write down this answer in German: "Let's meet tomorrow morning."

12) The cousin says: "Treffen wir uns bei mir zu Hause." Where are you going to meet?

13) While you're in town you decide to go and see a film. Eager to show off your
    linguistic talent you ask for two tickets. What would you say, in German?

14) Sort these words out into three columns, "der", "die" and "das".
    Auto Bus Flugzeug Fahrrad Motorrad
    Reisebus Schiff Straßenbahn U-Bahn Zug

15) Write sentences starting "Ich fahre mit dem / der ..." for each of these
    types of transport: a) underground   b) coach   c) car

16) How do you ask if there's a train going to Berlin, in German?

17) How do you ask which platform the train leaves from?

18) Ask for a return ticket, second class, to Freiburg.

Telephones

Even though phones are just the same in Germany, you still have to learn about them.

Telephone numbers — die Telefonnummer

German people say their telephone numbers in a different way. Make sure you can say your phone number and understand if people tell you theirs.

> telephone number:
> **die Telefonnummer**

Say your <u>phone number</u> in <u>groups of 2</u>, e.g. thirty-five, not three five.

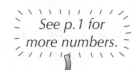
See p.1 for more numbers.

Meine Telefonnummer ist **fünfunddreißig, vierzig, zweiundzwanzig** .

= My telephone number is <u>35</u>, <u>40</u>, <u>22</u>.

Phoning people

Here's what you say when you <u>phone someone</u>:

Hallo! Hier spricht Ben. = Hello, it's Ben here.

Kann ich mit Kaspar sprechen? = Can I speak to Kaspar?

Hello! Can I speak to the Chancellor?

It's probably not a good idea to phone the Chancellor of Germany, but these phrases will help you if you want to speak to a German person on the phone. Make sure you learn them.

At the Post Office

Not many people send letters nowadays, but you're going to have to pretend you want to.

At the post office — Auf der Post

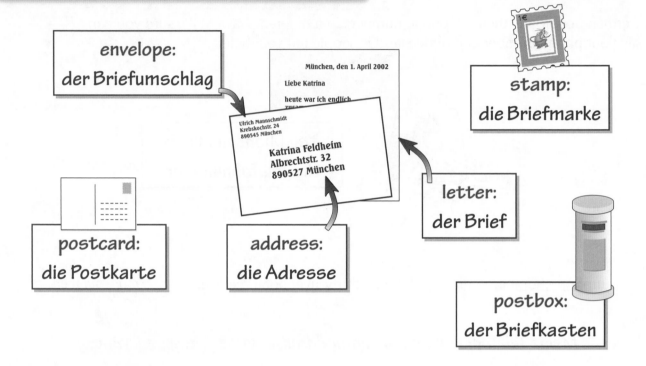

envelope:
der Briefumschlag

stamp:
die Briefmarke

postcard:
die Postkarte

address:
die Adresse

letter:
der Brief

postbox:
der Briefkasten

Buying a stamp

This is how you <u>ask</u> for a <u>stamp</u>:

a one-euro stamp: eine Ein-Euro-Briefmarke

Ich möchte *eine Zwei-Euro-Briefmarke*, bitte.   = I'd like a <u>two-euro stamp</u>, please.

If you <u>don't know</u> what kind of stamp you need, this is what to say:

Ich möchte einen Brief nach *Großbritannien* schicken.

= I'd like to send a letter to <u>Britain</u>.

Change "Großbritannien" to whatever country you need, e.g. "Frankreich". See p.94 for more countries.

Was kostet es?   = How much is that?

Make sure you know how to ask for a stamp

You might not think you'll ever write a letter, but you really do need to know this stuff. You might have to do a role play where you need to buy some stamps and post a letter. Learn it.

Informal Letters

This is the <u>letter-specific stuff</u> you need for KS3 German. Informal letters are on this page — that's letters to <u>penpals</u> and <u>friends</u>. It works for <u>postcards</u> too.

Start a letter with "Lieber / Liebe..." — "Dear..."

Use this <u>layout</u> for your <u>informal letters</u>. <u>Town</u> and <u>date</u> on the <u>right</u>, then <u>start</u> and <u>end</u> properly.

In a <u>real</u> letter to your penpal, you might want to say a bit about yourself too — look through the book, especially sections 2, 3 & 5.

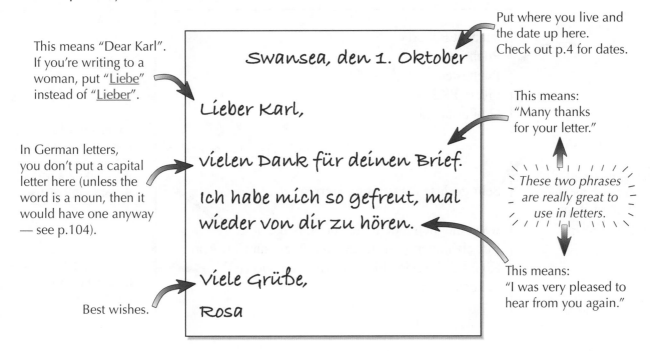

This means "Dear Karl". If you're writing to a woman, put "<u>Liebe</u>" instead of "<u>Lieber</u>".

In German letters, you don't put a capital letter here (unless the word is a noun, then it would have one anyway — see p.104).

Best wishes.

Put where you live and the date up here. Check out p.4 for dates.

This means: "Many thanks for your letter."

These two phrases are really great to use in letters.

This means: "I was very pleased to hear from you again."

> Swansea, den 1. Oktober
>
> Lieber Karl,
>
> Vielen Dank für deinen Brief.
>
> Ich habe mich so gefreut, mal wieder von dir zu hören.
>
> Viele Grüße,
>
> Rosa

Don't panic if you have to write a <u>postcard</u> — just do the same as for a short letter.

Other **phrases** to use in your **letters**

Here's a useful phrase you can bung in at the <u>start</u> of any informal letter.

Wie geht's? = How are you?

Stick this sentence in <u>just before</u> you sign off.

Schreib bald! = Write soon!

This is <u>another way</u> to sign off — you can use it <u>instead of</u> "Viele Grüße".

Bis bald. = See you soon.

Remember it's "Liebe" for a woman and "Lieber" for a man

Lots of useful phrases here. Practise using them by writing letters to all of your friends. Don't get caught out by starting with a capital letter (unless it's a noun of course).

Formal Letters

You need a formal letter when you write to book a hotel room, or for writing to a tourist office in Zurich or something. For more on hotel booking, see p.92.

Learn the **special phrases** for **formal letters**

3 things to learn here: 1) The layout (your full address top left); 2) How to start; 3) How to end.

Your name and full address go up here.

Put this if you don't know the person's name.
If you do know, put "Sehr geehrter Herr Bloggs" or "Sehr geehrte Frau Blah".

Yours sincerely.

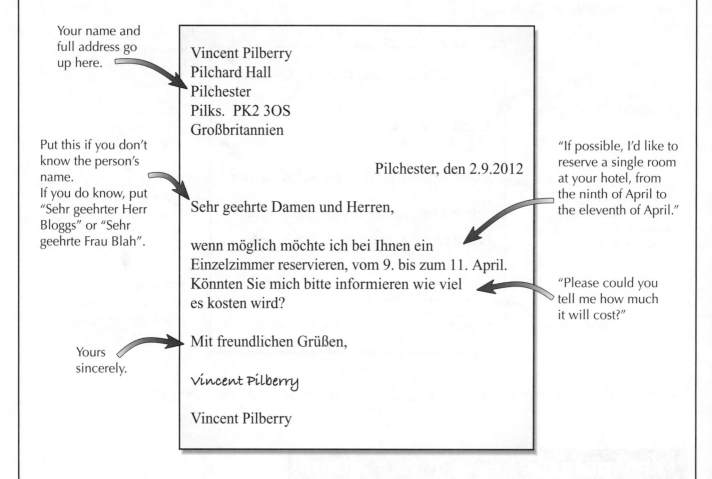

Vincent Pilberry
Pilchard Hall
Pilchester
Pilks. PK2 3OS
Großbritannien

Pilchester, den 2.9.2012

Sehr geehrte Damen und Herren,

wenn möglich möchte ich bei Ihnen ein Einzelzimmer reservieren, vom 9. bis zum 11. April. Könnten Sie mich bitte informieren wie viel es kosten wird?

Mit freundlichen Grüßen,

Vincent Pilberry

Vincent Pilberry

"If possible, I'd like to reserve a single room at your hotel, from the ninth of April to the eleventh of April."

"Please could you tell me how much it will cost?"

Another useful phrase

Here's another phrase you can stick in just before you sign off:

Vielen Dank im Voraus.   = Many thanks in advance.

You should be an expert on letter writing now

The phrases you need to use for a formal letter are very different to those for an informal one, so you have to learn all of them. You still don't use a capital letter after "Dear...," though.

Practice Questions

1 Write out your parts of this phone conversation, in German.
The bits in brackets tell you what to say.

Frau Schulz: *Hallo.*

  a) You: *[Hello. It's (your name) here. Can I speak to Katharina, please?]*

Frau Schulz: *Sie ist nicht hier.*

  b) You: *[Where is she, please?]*

Frau Schulz: *Sie ist in der Bibliothek. Was ist Ihre Telefonnummer?*

  c) You: *[My telephone number is 763715. Thanks, Mrs Schulz.]*

2 Write out these informal letter phrases in English.
Choose from the phrases in the box.

a) Viele Grüße.

b) Schreib bald.

c) Vielen Dank für deinen Brief.

d) Bis bald.

e) Wie geht's?

> Best wishes.
>
> How are you?
>
> See you soon.
>
> Write soon.
>
> Many thanks for your letter.

3 Read this letter, then answer the questions (in **English**).

> Wien, den 20. Mai
>
> Liebe Sam,
>
> ich habe mich so gefreut, mal wieder von dir zu hören.
>
> Was ist dein Lieblingsfach? Mein Lieblingsfach ist Kunst, weil sie einfach ist. Ich hasse Naturwissenschaften, weil sie langweilig und schwierig sind. Welches Schulfach hasst du?
>
> Schreib bald!
>
> Lukas

a) Is Sam a boy or a girl?

b) What is the first thing Lukas says, after the "Liebe Sam" bit?

c) Why does Lukas hate science?

d) What does Lukas tell Sam to do at the end of his letter?

4 Write a formal letter in German, using the information given below and your own name and address. Use today's date.

- You're writing to Mr Neumann at Hotel Dieter.

- Say you'd like to reserve a double room from the 23rd of October to the 28th of October.

  Hint: double room = das Doppelzimmer

- Ask how much it will cost.

- Say "Many thanks in advance".

- Put "Yours sincerely" and your name.

Summary Questions

Use these questions to find out what you've got sussed and what you haven't. Read through these pages again and try and answer all these questions. Then go back through the pages to check your answers. If you got any wrong, go back and try again.

1) Complete this phrase, in German, writing the numbers out in words:
   "My telephone number is..."

2) Say these phone numbers in German:

   a) 445566

   b) 346742

   c) 986345

   d) 354667

3) You're phoning your German friend, Stefan. How do you ask to speak to him?

4) What do the following mean in English?

   a) der Briefumschlag

   b) der Briefkasten

   c) die Briefmarke

   d) der Brief

5) In a German post office, how would you ask for a one-euro stamp?

6) In German, write out how you'd say you want to send a postcard to Scotland.

7) If you were writing a letter to your German friend, Heidi, whereabouts on the paper would you write the date? What else would you write there?

8) Write a short letter to your Austrian penfriend, Dagmar (a girl).
   Thank her for her letter, ask her how she is, and tell her to write soon.

9) How do you say "I was very pleased to hear from you again", in German?

10) What does 'Bis bald' mean in English?

11) In German, how do you start a formal letter if you don't know the person's name?

12) How do you write "many thanks in advance" in German?

Weather and Seasons

This is the <u>question</u> you'll get asked about the weather:

Wie ist das Wetter? = What's the weather like?

Say what the weather's like — "es ist..."

These <u>nine</u> types of weather all start "<u>es ist</u>" ("it is").

 es ist schön
= it's nice weather

es ist schlecht
= it's bad weather

 es ist heiß
= it's hot

es ist kalt
= it's cold

 es ist sonnig
= it's sunny

es ist wolkig
= it's cloudy

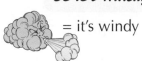 **es ist windig**
= it's windy

 es ist stürmisch
= it's stormy

es ist neblig
= it's foggy

<u>Raining</u> and <u>snowing</u> are <u>different</u>. There's <u>no</u> "ist" in the sentence.

es regnet
= it's raining

es schneit
= it's snowing

The seasons — die Jahreszeiten

["die Jahreszeit" = season]

Ah, the seasons. Only <u>four</u> of them to learn, and <u>two</u> of them are <u>easy</u>. Can't say fairer than that.

| spring:
 der Frühling | summer:
 der Sommer | autumn:
 der Herbst | winter:
 der Winter |

Learn this stuff — or you won't have the neblig-iest

There's something great about those words for seasons — they're <u>all</u> "der" words. So why is "Jahreszeit" a "die" word... Ours is not to reason why, but mainly to learn German vocab.

Holidays

Holidays are a bit like weather in a way — they're a good ice-breaker for talking to people you don't really know. They're also a favourite topic in KS3 German.

Talk about where you normally go on holiday

The bits on the left are the questions you could get asked about holidays.
The bits on the right are your answers — change the underlined bits to match your own holiday.

Wohin fährst du normalerweise in Urlaub?

= Where do you go on holiday normally?

Normalerweise fahre ich nach Wales.

= Normally, I go to Wales.

For other countries, see p.94.

For other people, see p.16.

Mit wem fährst du in Urlaub?

= Who do you go on holiday with?

Ich fahre mit meiner Mutter.

= I go with my mother.

After "mit" you use "meiner" for a female relative and "meinem" for a male one. This is the dative (see p.114).

Wie lange machst du Urlaub?

= How long do you go on holiday for?

Ich mache eine Woche Urlaub.

= I go for one week.

For other times, see p.3.

For other places, see p.91.

Wo übernachtest du normalerweise?

= Where do you normally stay?

Ich übernachte in einem Hotel.

= I stay in a hotel.

"einem" is dative, see p.115.

Was machst du?

= What do you do?

Ich gehe an den Strand.

= I go to the beach.

For other things to do, see p.69.

Wie ist das Wetter normalerweise?

= What's the weather like normally?

Es regnet.

= It rains.

For other weather, see p.89.

Learn the questions as well as the answers

If you don't know the questions you won't be able to understand what people say to you, and you won't be able to ask them stuff either. Knuckle down and learn both bits.

Hotels and Camping

There's plenty of cracking vocab on this page. Make sure you <u>learn it all</u>.

Learn these **places to stay**

It's all a question of how much you want to <u>pay</u> per night,
and whether you want <u>ants</u> in your shoes when you wake up.

campsite:
der Campingplatz

hotel:
das Hotel

youth hostel:
die Jugendherberge

At the hotel — **im Hotel**

The most important stuff to learn about hotels is the <u>different types of rooms</u>:

room:
ein Zimmer

single room:
ein Einzelzimmer

double room:
ein Doppelzimmer

Ein Zimmer mit Bad .

= A room with a <u>bath</u>.

a shower:	Dusche
a balcony:	Balkon
a bathroom:	Badezimmer

There's some other stuff you need to learn too:

telephone:
das Telefon

toilet:
die Toilette

dining room:
der Speisesaal

key:
der Schlüssel

This stuff is all super useful

This is top-notch KS3 German vocabulary. Once you've remembered all the words for things
to do with hotels, you need to know how to use them. That's where the next page comes in...

Booking Accommodation

There's a lot of learning to do on this page. Take it <u>one bit at a time</u> — easy does it.

Booking a hotel room — tell them **what** and **when**

Mmm. Booking a room is <u>easier</u> than it seems — just fiddle these phrases to say the <u>dates</u> / <u>number of nights</u> you want. Make sure you read the <u>questions</u> so you'll understand them.

① *Haben Sie Zimmer frei?* = Have you any rooms free?

② *Ich möchte ein Einzelzimmer.* = I would like <u>a single room</u>.

> *a double room:* ein Doppelzimmer

Für wie viele Nächte? = For how many nights?

③ *Ich möchte hier eine Nacht bleiben.* = I would like to stay here <u>one night</u>.

> *two nights:* zwei Nächte
> *one week:* eine Woche
> *two weeks:* zwei Wochen

For other numbers, see p.1.

Von wann bis wann möchten Sie bleiben? = When would you like to stay?

> *fourth of May:* vierten Mai

④ *Ich möchte vom ersten Juni bis zum zweiten Juni bleiben.* = I would like to stay from the <u>first of June</u> to the <u>second of June</u>.

> *eleventh of May:* elften Mai

"First", "second", "fourth", etc. are all on p.1. Watch out — they end in "n" in this sentence (it's dative, see p.115).

⑤ *Was kostet das?* = How much is that?

Excellent — now you can go on holiday to Germany

This page gives you all the phrases you'll need to book a hotel in Germany. Now you've just got to learn it all — unless you want to wander round clutching this book of course.

More Camping

Some people prefer camping to staying in a hotel — it's cheaper, you get lots of fresh air and there's a bit less vocabulary you need to know before you go. Here goes...

At the campsite — auf dem Campingplatz

These are the <u>campsite</u> bits you have to know. Watch the <u>spelling</u> — they're <u>odd</u>.

tent:
das Zelt

pitch (space for a tent):
der Platz

sleeping bag:
der Schlafsack

caravan:
der Wohnwagen

drinking water:
das Trinkwasser

Booking into a campsite — don't ask for a room

The <u>first bit</u> of booking into a <u>campsite</u> is <u>different</u> from a hotel (no rooms in a campsite, see).

Haben Sie Plätze frei?   = Have you any pitches free?

Ich möchte einen Platz für ein Zelt.   = I would like a pitch <u>for a tent</u>.

> *for a caravan:*   für einen Wohnwagen

Booking a place at a campsite is easy once you've learnt this stuff

Write out the phrases you need for getting a place at a campsite. Then write them out again, and again till you can do it without looking. Then you can go and look for your tent pegs.

Countries

These are the countries you need for <u>KS3 German</u>. Obviously there are more out there — if you're <u>desperate</u>, you can look them up in a dictionary. But make sure you <u>learn all these ones first</u>.

European countries — europäische Länder

["das Land" = country]

das Vereinigte Königreich = the United Kingdom   *Großbritannien* = Great Britain

People speak German in Germany, Austria and Switzerland.

Scotland: **Schottland**

Northern Ireland: **Nordirland**

England: **England**

Holland: **Holland**

Germany: **Deutschland**

The Republic of Ireland: **Irland**

Wales: **Wales**

Belgium: **Belgien**

Austria: **Österreich**

France: **Frankreich**

Switzerland: **die Schweiz**

Spain: **Spanien**

Italy: **Italien**

Portugal: **Portugal**

Don't flag — keep going till you've learnt them all

"Das Vereinigte Königreich" is one of the trickiest phrases in this book, but maybe I've just got a mental block about it... Learn <u>all</u> the countries. You never know when you might need them.

Nationalities

If someone asks <u>where you're from</u> you can just say "I live in Alaska" — it's "Ich wohne in Alaska".

Saying where you live — "ich wohne in..."

Pick the one of these that's for where <u>you</u> live, and <u>learn it</u>.

"ich wohne in" + COUNTRY

Ich wohne in England.　= I live in England.　　*Ich wohne in Wales.*　= I live in Wales.

Ich wohne in Nordirland.　= I live in Northern Ireland.

Ich wohne in Schottland.　= I live in Scotland.

Saying your nationality — "ich bin..."

This is how you put the sentence together:

"ich bin" + NATIONALITY　　*Ich bin Engländer.*　= I am English.

You need to learn all the UK nationalities:

English:	Engländer(in)	*Northern Irish:*	Nordirländer(in)
Welsh:	Waliser(in)	*Scottish:*	Schotte/Schottin

They all end with "in" if you're female.

Five foreign nationalities

Five more nationalities that can be tacked on after "Ich bin...":

Spanish:	Spanier(in)	*French:*	Franzose/Französin
Italian:	Italiener(in)	*German:*	Deutscher/Deutsche
Irish:	Ire/Irin		

Ich bin Engländer. Ich wohne in England.

This stuff is nice and simple. You need to know how to say where you're from and where you live, but you also need to know the vocabulary for other nationalities too.

Practice Questions

Track 15   <u>Listening Question</u>

1   Listen to this weather report. Match each of the countries marked on the map to the type of weather mentioned (labelled 1-8 below). Some countries have more than one type of weather.

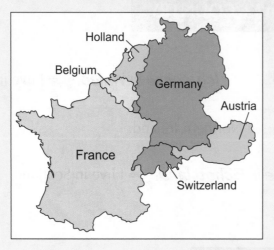

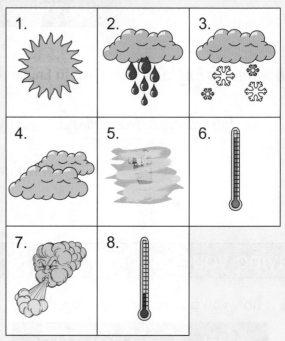

Track 16

2   Listen to this phone conversation in which a customer is booking campsite accommodation. Write down whether each of these sentences is true or false.

a)   The customer has a caravan.

b)   They want to stay for two weeks.

c)   The campsite has no space in August.

d)   There are two children in the family.

e)   They will have to pay extra to bring the cat.

3   Copy and complete your bits of this conversation about holidays in German.

Karl: Wohin fährst du normalerweise in Urlaub?

You: ....   [Normally I go to France.]

Karl: Mit wem fährst du?

You: ....   [I go with my aunt.]

Karl: Wo übernachtest du normalerweise?

You: ....   [I stay in a youth hostel.]

Practice Questions

4   Write out, in German, how you would describe these rooms.
I've done the first one for you.

a)   +

c)   +

Ein Einzelzimmer mit Balkon.

b) +

d) +

5   These are words that you will need about hotels, hostels and camping.
Write out the English meaning for each one. I've done the first one for you.

a)   der Campingplatz   *campsite*

b)   die Jugendherberge

c)   der Platz

d)   der Wohnwagen

e)   der Schlafsack

f)   das Trinkwasser

6   Write out the names of these countries in German.

a)   Germany

c)   Northern Ireland

e)   The United Kingdom

b)   Scotland

d)   Great Britain

f)   France

7   Imagine that you are each of these people. Write out how they would describe
their nationality in German. I've done the first one for you.

a)   James   *Ich bin Engländer.*

b)   Charley

c)   Claire

d)   Iryna

e)   Ian

f)   Helen

HINT: Watch out for whether it
should be masculine or feminine.

Summary Questions

Ee, by gum, holidays are grand. No work, no worries, plenty of fun... But the downside of being on holiday is you don't have the honour and privilege of doing KS3 German. Make sure you get everything out of this section — use these questions to check what's sunk in, and what you need to go over again. That means: do the questions once from memory, check what you got right, then keep doing them till you get them all right. Well worth the effort.

1) Write these weather phrases out in German:
   a) "it's cold"   c) "it's raining"
   b) "it's sunny"   d) "it's nice weather"

2) Write out what these sentences mean in English:
   a) Es ist schlecht.   c) Es ist stürmisch.
   b) Es ist heiß.   d) Es schneit.

3) Describe today's weather in German.

4) These are three of the seasons. "der Herbst, der Winter, der Sommer".
   What do they mean in English? Write, in German, the name of the missing season.

5) Holidays — how would you say this in German?
   "Normally, I go to Belgium. I go with my father. I go for two weeks.
   I stay in a hotel. I go to the beach."

6) Imagine you're trying to book into Hotel Innsbruck.
   How would you ask if they have any rooms free?

7) How would you say these in German?
   a) I'd like a single room.
   b) I would like to stay one week.
   c) Which date is it for?

8) What does this mean in English? *"Haben Sie Plätze frei?"*

9) How do you say these in German?
   a) key   d) toilet
   b) hotel   e) dining room
   c) tent   f) single room

10) What are these countries called in English?
   a) Belgien   b) die Schweiz   c) Österreich   d) Spanien

11) Write these country names out in German:
   a) England   b) Italy   c) Holland

12) Your penfriend Dieter says *"Ich wohne in Deutschland. Ich bin Deutscher."*
   a) Where does Dieter live?
   b) What nationality is Dieter?
   c) Write out your own version, to say where you live and what your nationality is.
   d) Write out a version for Rafael Nadal, who is Spanish and lives in Spain.

Opinions

This page is all about speaking your mind. Learn these phrases so you can <u>say what you think</u>.

'I like' and 'I don't like'

Use these four phrases to say what you like and what you don't like.

① *Ich mag...* = I like...

② *Ich liebe...* = I love...

Ich mag Kaffee. = I like coffee.

Ich liebe Kaffee. = I love coffee.

③ *Ich mag... nicht.* = I don't like...

④ *Ich hasse...* = I hate...

Ich mag Schildkröten <u>nicht</u>.

= I don't like tortoises.

Ich hasse Schildkröten.

= I hate tortoises.

"<u>Nicht</u>" always goes at <u>the end</u> of the phrase.

You can also say 'I like' using **gern**

"<u>Gern</u>" is a handy wee word for saying you <u>like doing something</u>.

1) Write down the <u>verb</u> you want. (See p.123 for 'what is a verb?')

Ich schwimme gern.

= I like swimming.

2) Add <u>gern</u> here — <u>straight after</u> the verb.

Here are some more examples:

Ich schlafe gern.

= I like sleeping.

Ich esse gern Spaghetti.

= I like eating spaghetti.

Ich mag Grammatik

Ahh — grammar. You might find it a bit scary, but good grammar is really important. Without it, your German won't make any sense. What a good job I'm here to help you with it.

Opinions

You don't just have to say what you like and dislike — you need to be able to <u>describe</u> things too.

Use describing words to say what you think

THING + IST / SIND + DESCRIBING WORD

1) Start with the <u>thing</u> you want to describe — a film, a person, a pair of shoes...

2) Then put <u>ist</u> for "is" — or <u>sind</u> for "are".

3) Finish off with a <u>describing word</u>. There are loads in the box at the bottom of this page.

Examples

Kochen ist langweilig.

= Cooking is boring.

Zeitungen sind interessant.

= Newspapers are interesting.

Basketball ist toll.

= Basketball is great.

good:	gut	*super:*	super
not good:	nicht gut	*wonderful:*	wunderbar
bad:	schlecht	*great:*	toll
interesting:	interessant	*tiring:*	anstrengend / ermüdend
easy:	leicht / einfach	*fun:*	lustig
hard:	schwer / schwierig	*daft:*	doof
stupid:	dumm	*fantastic:*	fantastisch
nice:	schön	*totally brilliant:*	einfach Klasse

Describing words help you, er... describe things

Describing words are great, but make sure you learn them properly. Otherwise you might get mixed up and accidentally say maths is great and German is stupid, and I wouldn't want that.

Asking Questions

If you want to be able to have a conversation in German, you need to be able to <u>ask questions</u>.

The words have a funny order in questions

Most of the time in German, the <u>I / you / he / they</u> bit comes <u>before</u> the verb.

> ***Du heißt Spartacus.***   = You are called Spartacus.

> **In a question the verb comes first**

There's more on verbs on p.123.

> ***Heißt du Spartacus?***   = Are you called Spartacus?

You can make questions by changing the **word order**

This makes the type of question that gets you a YES or NO answer —
like "Do you like crumpets?" or "Shall we go to the pictures?". All you do is
switch the <u>verb</u> and the <u>I / you / he / they</u> bit, exactly like in the example above.

> ***Englisch ist interessant.***   = English is interesting.

> ***Ist Englisch interessant?***   = Is English interesting?

> ***Der Hund stinkt.***   = The dog smells.

> ***Stinkt der Hund?***   = Does the dog smell?

Put the verb first when you're asking a question
Always, always remember to switch the word order. Oh, and remember the question mark of
course. Once you've got those done you can sit and look smug. If you like that kind of thing.

Asking Questions

There's more than one way to ask a question in German. You learnt the easy way on the previous page — this page is all about the ever-so-slightly trickier way.

You can make a question by using a **question word**

1) Start by <u>changing the word order</u>...

du trinkst ➡ **trinkst du**

= you are drinking = are you drinking

2) ...then stick a <u>question word</u> in at the beginning.

<u>Was</u> trinkst du?

= <u>What</u> are you drinking?

Here are some more examples:

<u>Wo</u> spielst du Tennis? = <u>Where</u> do you play tennis?

<u>Warum</u> magst du Sonja? = <u>Why</u> do you like Sonja?

Learn these question words

These are the German <u>question words</u> you need to know.
They all start with <u>W</u> — a bit like English.

Wer? = Who?

Warum? = Why?

Wo? = Where?

Was? = What?

Wann? = When?

Wohin? = Where to?

Wie? = How?

Wer? Was? Wo? Wann?
Questions, questions. Now you've got an army of question words up your sleeve, you could go out and ask someone anything you like in German. Well, maybe not anything.

Practice Questions

1   Write these sentences out in German.

    a)   I like tea. [tea = der Tee]

    b)   I love Maths. [Maths = die Mathe]

    c)   I don't like coffee. [coffee = Kaffee]

    d)   I hate goldfish. [goldfish = die Goldfische]

    e)   I like German. [German = Deutsch]

    f)   I don't like science. [science = Naturwissenschaften]

2   Write the following out in German. [Hint: history = Geschichte]

    a)   History is great.   d)   History is good.

    b)   History is tiring.   e)   History is fantastic.

    c)   History is hard.

3   Here's a load of statements. Change them into simple yes/no questions.
Then translate your questions into English. I've done the first one for you.

    a)   Du möchtest einen Apfel. [You would like an apple.]
        Möchtest du einen Apfel? (Would you like an apple?)

    b)   Er heißt Romeo. [He is called Romeo.]

    c)   Du hast einen Hund. [You have a dog.]

    d)   Wir lernen Deutsch. [We learn German.]

    e)   Es gibt hier in der Nähe ein Schloss. [There is a castle near here.]

4   Match the German words on the left with their English meanings on the right.

    1. Wann?   a. What?

    2. Warum?   b. Why?

    3. Was?   c. How?

    4. Wer?   d. Where?

    5. Wie?   e. When?

    6. Wo?   f. Where (to)?

    7. Wohin?   g. Who?

Nouns — Capital Letters and Gender

You need to understand this page, which means you need to know what a <u>noun</u> is:
A noun is a word for a <u>thing</u>, a <u>person</u> or a <u>place</u>. So "pen", "Julia" and "Berlin" <u>are</u> all nouns.
But "sideways" and "big" <u>are not</u> nouns. Ask "teach" if you're baffled.

Every German noun has a **capital letter**

In English, only <u>some</u> nouns have a capital, e.g. Doris, November, Greenland.
But in <u>German</u>, <u>absolutely every noun</u> has a capital letter. <u>Every single one</u>.

Kuli	**Zug**	**Hund**	**Banane**	**Wahrheit**
= pen	= train	= dog	= banana	= truth

See, they've all got capital letters.

Every German noun is **masculine**, **feminine** or **neuter**

Every German noun is either <u>masculine</u>, <u>feminine</u> or <u>neuter</u>. Don't ask me why.
When you're writing, you need to <u>know</u> whether each noun is <u>masc.</u>, <u>fem.</u> or <u>neut.</u> because it
affects the <u>words around them</u>. For example, you need different words for "<u>the</u>". Look:

How to say "the" — **der**, **die** and **das**

In German, there are <u>three</u> words to say "the". (Sounds weird, but there you go.)
It's a different word for <u>masculine</u>, <u>feminine</u> or <u>neuter</u>. <u>Plural</u> words are always "<u>die</u>".

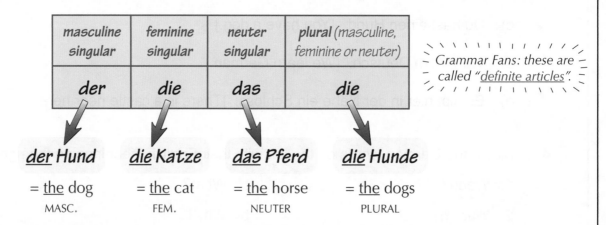

masculine singular	feminine singular	neuter singular	plural *(masculine, feminine or neuter)*
der	*die*	*das*	*die*

Grammar Fans: these are called "<u>definite articles</u>".

<u>**der**</u> **Hund**	<u>**die**</u> **Katze**	<u>**das**</u> **Pferd**	<u>**die**</u> **Hunde**
= <u>the</u> dog	= <u>the</u> cat	= <u>the</u> horse	= <u>the</u> dogs
MASC.	FEM.	NEUTER	PLURAL

So, it's no good just knowing the German words for things — you have to know whether
each one's <u>masculine</u>, <u>feminine</u> or <u>neuter</u> too. Each time you <u>learn</u> a <u>word</u>, remember the
<u>der</u>, <u>die</u> or <u>das</u> to go with it — don't think "dog = Hund", think "dog = <u>der</u> Hund".

Know your "der" from your "die" and your "das"
Now you might think it's silly having three words for "the". But the Germans love it, and "the"
is a pretty important word, so you can't just avoid using it. You'll have to learn them sometime.

Nouns — Plurals

Plurals in German can be a bit of a pain. This page gives you a few handy hints on how to find out what the plural of a word is. Go on, give it a try — you might even enjoy it...

Plurals are tricky

English plurals are easy — you usually add an 's' (e.g. one boy, two boy<u>s</u>).
In German, there's no one rule for plurals.

There are two things you can do to make sure you get a plural right:

> 1) learn each plural off by heart when you learn each word,
>
> OR 2) look it up in a dictionary.

You can look up plurals in a **dictionary**

Your dictionary might have the plural written out, like this:

> **shoe** NOUN *der Schuh (PL die Schuhe)*

> ***song*** NOUN *das Lied (PL die Lieder)*

> ***mouse*** NOUN *die Maus (PL die Mäuse)*

der Schuh

Some nouns need an umlaut when they are plural. Depending on the word, it might have letters added to the end too (e.g. the "e" in Mäuse).

Or it might have the ending to add in brackets:

> ***shoe*** NOUN *der Schuh (-e)*

> ***song*** NOUN *das Lied (-er)*

> ***mouse*** NOUN *die Maus (⸚e)*

die Schuhe

This means an umlaut is added to one of the vowels (usually the first one) and an "e" is added on the end.

Try and learn the plurals of words you use a lot
Dictionaries are great for finding out a plural, but you won't always have a dictionary handy. Try learning the plurals of words you use a lot so you don't have to keep looking them up.

How to Say "A"

This sounds like a lovely simple page. And it is... sort of. In German, you say "a" differently depending on what follows it. It's a bit like "der", "die" and "das".

How to say "a" — **ein, eine, ein**

It's easy in <u>English</u> — there's just one word for "a". You can say "a man", "a woman", whatever.

In <u>German</u>, "a" can be "<u>ein</u>" or "<u>eine</u>".
It depends whether the thing you're talking about is <u>masculine</u>, <u>feminine</u> or <u>neuter</u>.

<u>Learn</u> this table <u>off by heart</u>. It's the only way.

The German Words for "A":

masculine singular	feminine singular	neuter singular
ein	*eine*	*ein*

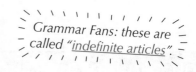

Grammar Fans: these are called "<u>indefinite articles</u>".

Examples

<u>ein</u> Hund

= <u>a</u> dog
MASC.

<u>ein</u> Pullover

= <u>a</u> jumper
MASC.

<u>eine</u> Katze

= <u>a</u> cat
FEM.

<u>eine</u> Bluse

= <u>a</u> blouse
FEM.

<u>ein</u> Pferd

= <u>a</u> horse
NEUTER

<u>ein</u> Kleid

= <u>a</u> dress
NEUTER

Only use "eine" for feminine words

"A" causes a lot of trouble for such a little word. You need to learn these rules, but the right ending also depends on what part of the sentence you're talking about (see pages 112-115).

How to Say "My" and "Your"

"Mein" means "<u>my</u>", and lucky for you it has the <u>same endings</u> as "ein".

My, Your, His, Her — saying whose it is

Right. You should be getting the hang of this by now:

1) In <u>German</u>, there is more than one word for "<u>my</u>".
2) It changes to match the thing it's describing — <u>masculine</u>, <u>feminine</u>, <u>neuter</u> or <u>plural</u>.
3) <u>Learn</u> this table. It follows the same basic pattern as "ein" (on the previous page).

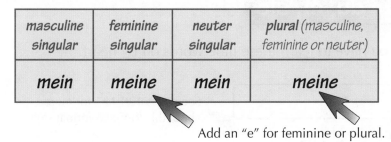

masculine singular	feminine singular	neuter singular	plural (masculine, feminine or neuter)
mein	**meine**	**mein**	**meine**

Grammar Fans: these are called "<u>possessive adjectives</u>".

Add an "e" for feminine or plural.

Here are some <u>examples</u>:

<u>mein</u> Hund   **<u>meine</u> Katze**   **<u>mein</u> Pferd**   **<u>meine</u> Pferde**

= <u>my</u> dog   = <u>my</u> cat   = <u>my</u> horse   = <u>my</u> horses

MASC.   FEM.   NEUTER   PLURAL

This is the <u>complete list</u> of the "my", "your", "his" type words.
They follow the <u>same pattern</u> as "mein" above — you <u>add an "e" for feminine or plural</u>.

mein	my
dein	your (informal singular)
sein	his
ihr	her
sein	its
unser	our
euer	your (informal plural)
Ihr	your (formal singular or plural)
ihr	their

See pages 120-121 for more about this formal/informal stuff.

Here are some <u>examples</u>:

<u>unser</u> Hund

= <u>our</u> dog
MASC.

<u>unsere</u> Katze

= <u>our</u> cat
FEM.

Learn these possessive adjectives
These words make all the difference when it comes to making yourself understood when you're speaking German. If you learn them now, you won't have to worry about them later.

Pronouns — "I", "You", "He", "They"...

Pronouns are words that replace nouns — they're words like "you", "she" or "they". For example:

*Frank is playing cards with
Jessica. He is about to lose.*

"He" is a pronoun. It means you don't have to say "Frank" again.

I, you, he, she — ich, du, er, sie

There's no getting round it — you have to learn these little words off by heart.

ich	I
du	you (informal singular)
er	he/it
sie	she/it
es	it
wir	we
ihr	you (informal plural)
Sie	you (formal singular or plural)
sie	they

See pages 120-121 for more about this formal/informal stuff.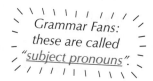

Grammar Fans: these are called "subject pronouns".

Examples

Daniela und Hans essen Brot *sie essen Brot*

= Daniela and Hans eat bread

= they eat bread

Matthias ist Deutscher *er ist Deutscher*

= Matthias is German

= he is German

Don't get "er" and "sie" mixed up or you might offend someone

"Sie" appears quite a lot on this page. That doesn't mean you can just plump for "sie" and hope it's correct. You need to learn all the different subject pronouns so you get it right every time.

Pronouns — "It"

Now it's time for "it". Just like everything else in German, "it" can be said more than one way.

There are three words for "it" — **er, sie** and **es**

Look at the green table on the previous page. In German there are <u>three words</u> for "<u>it</u>".
Learn this <u>easy</u> way to remember which word to use — they <u>rhyme</u>:

> **"DER" is replaced by "ER".**
> **"DIE" is replaced by "SIE".**
> **"DAS" is replaced by "ES".**

Examples

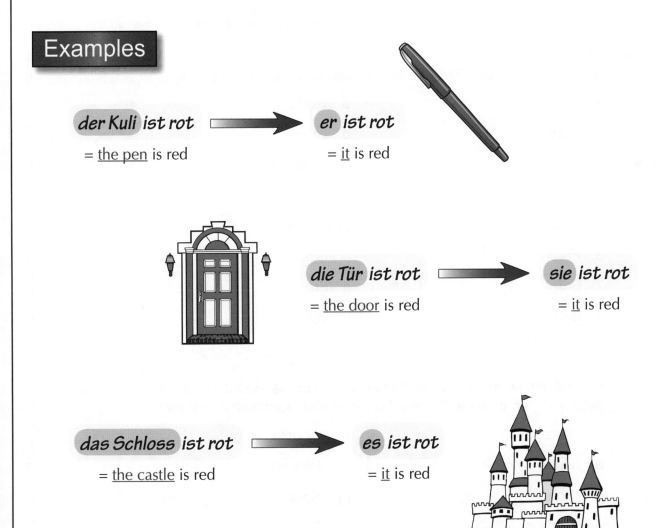

der Kuli *ist rot* ➡ *er* *ist rot*

= <u>the pen</u> is red = <u>it</u> is red

die Tür *ist rot* ➡ *sie* *ist rot*

= <u>the door</u> is red = <u>it</u> is red

das Schloss *ist rot* ➡ *es* *ist rot*

= <u>the castle</u> is red = <u>it</u> is red

Learn the rules for the three "it" words
Once you know whether the noun you are talking about is masculine, feminine or neuter, use
the rule in the blue box to work out which word for "it" you need. Nice and simple, hurrah!

Practice Questions

1 Copy and complete this table. Put the nouns in the correct columns, depending on whether each is a der, die or das word (masculine, feminine or neuter). I've done one for you. HINT: They're all singular, not plural.

Pferd   Hund   Katze
Freundin
Schuh
Bruder   Kuli   Tante
Schwester   Onkel
Cousine   Knie   Vater
Haus   Ohr

DER (masc.)	DIE (fem.)	DAS (neut.)
	Schwester	

HINT: Check in a dictionary if you're not sure whether it's masculine, feminine or neuter.

2 Match the singular words on the left with their plurals on the right.

1. Katze
2. Hund
3. Schuh
4. Banane
5. Tante
6. Freund
7. Sofa
8. Bett

a. Sofas
b. Hunde
c. Bananen
d. Betten
e. Katzen
f. Schuhe
g. Freunde
h. Tanten

3 Write these nouns out, adding the correct German word for "a" ("ein" or "eine"), depending on whether the word is masculine, feminine or neuter.

a) Katze
b) Hund
c) Schuh
d) Banane
e) Tante

f) Cousin
g) Freund
h) Sofa
i) Bett

Practice Questions

4 This time, write the nouns out adding the correct word for "my", depending on whether they are masculine, feminine or neuter.

a) Pferd

b) Schuh

c) Kuli

d) Hund

e) Katze

f) Onkel

g) Schwester

h) Bruder

i) Vater

j) Freundin

k) Tante

l) Cousin

m) Haus

n) Ohr

o) Knie

5 Write these out in German. HINT: The words for dog, brother etc. are all in Q4.

a) my dog

b) their brother

c) my uncle

d) her friend (female)

e) our cousin (male)

f) my horse

g) his father

h) our cat

6 Write out these sentences, replacing the underlined bits with the appropriate pronoun (I, you, him…). I've done the first one for you.

a) <u>Miriam und Peter</u> trinken Wasser. [<u>Miriam and Peter</u> drink water.]

Sie trinken Wasser.

b) <u>Peter, Maria und ich</u> haben lange Haare. [<u>Peter, Maria and I</u> have long hair.]

c) <u>Roger</u> ist hier. [<u>Roger</u> is here.]

d) <u>Meine Tante</u> kauft Brot. [<u>My aunt</u> buys bread.]

e) Wie alt ist <u>Peter</u>? [How old is <u>Peter</u>?]

7 Write out these sentences, replacing the underlined words with one of the pronouns "sie","er" or "es". I've done the first one for you.

a) <u>Die Katze</u> ist süß. *Sie ist süß.*

b) <u>Der Hund</u> ist groß.

c) <u>Die Kuh</u> ist dumm.

d) <u>Der Kuli</u> ist grün.

e) <u>Das Pferd</u> ist schwarz.

The Accusative Case

In German you sometimes have to change the <u>endings</u> of words. This page is about changing <u>der</u>.

Sentences can have a **subject** and an **object**

<u>Every</u> sentence has a <u>subject</u>.

> **SUBJECT = whoever (or whatever) is doing something**

Example:
<u>Norma</u> sang.

Some sentences have an <u>object</u> too.

> **OBJECT = whoever or whatever is having something done to it**

Example:
Norma sang <u>a song</u>.

When a word is the <u>object</u> you sometimes have to <u>change the ending</u> of "a" or "the". This is called using the <u>accusative case</u>. Read on...

PICKY RULE 1: Change **der** to **den** for the object

1) When a <u>masculine</u> word (e.g. <u>der Wagen</u>) is the object, change "<u>der</u>" to "<u>den</u>".

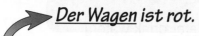

Der Wagen ist rot.

= <u>The car</u> is red.

<u>Wagen</u> is the <u>subject</u> here so leave it as "der Wagen".

Paul kauft <u>den Wagen</u>.

= Paul buys <u>the car</u>.

Here <u>Wagen</u> is the <u>object</u>. Change <u>der</u> to <u>den</u>.

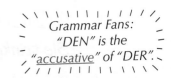

Grammar Fans: "DEN" is the "accusative" of "DER".

2) <u>Das</u> stays the same, for <u>neuter</u> words.

Das Hemd ist rot.

= <u>The shirt</u> is red.

Paul kauft <u>das Hemd</u>.

= Paul buys <u>the shirt</u>.

3) <u>Die</u> stays the same too, for <u>feminine</u> words...

Die Tomate ist rot.

= <u>The tomato</u> is red.

Paul kauft <u>die Tomate</u>.

= Paul buys <u>the tomato</u>.

...and for <u>plurals</u>.

Die Handschuhe sind rot.

= <u>The gloves</u> are red.

Paul kauft <u>die Handschuhe</u>.

= Paul buys <u>the gloves</u>.

The Accusative Case

PICKY RULE 2: Change **ein** to **einen**

1) When a <u>masculine</u> word is the object, you change "<u>ein</u>" to "<u>einen</u>" (just like you change "<u>der</u>" to "<u>den</u>", see previous page).

Paul hat <u>einen Wagen</u>.

= Paul has a car.

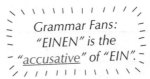

Grammar Fans: "EINEN" is the "<u>accusative</u>" of "EIN".

2) "<u>Mein</u>" and "<u>kein</u>" have exactly the same endings as "<u>ein</u>"— give them an extra "<u>en</u>" too.

Er hat <u>keinen Wagen</u>.   = He has <u>not</u> got <u>a car</u>.

Er kauft <u>meinen Wagen</u>.   = He's buying <u>my car</u>.

3) "<u>Ein</u>", "<u>mein</u>" and "<u>kein</u>"stay the same for a neuter word.

Paul hat <u>ein Hemd</u>.   = Paul has <u>a shirt</u>.

4) "<u>Eine</u>", "<u>meine</u>" and "<u>keine</u>" don't change either.

Paul hat <u>meine Tomate</u>.   = Paul has <u>my tomato</u>.

> **REMEMBER: "der" and the other little words that go with "der" words get EN on the end. For "die" and "das" words there's NO CHANGE to the endings.**

"Ein" only changes to "einen" if it's a masculine noun

This works in exactly the same way as "der" and "den". Watch out though — if the "ein" is in front of a neuter word, it <u>doesn't</u> change to "einen". Just something to keep you on your toes...

The Dative Case

Now here's the page you've all been waiting for... the dative case. Take a deep breath and begin...

Use the DATIVE after these words

The dative's another set of <u>special endings</u>. You put the <u>dative</u> of "<u>der</u>", "<u>ein</u>", "<u>mein</u>" and "<u>kein</u>" after these words to say where something or someone is:

in	in
von	from
auf	on (top of)
an	at / on
mit	with
gegenüber	opposite
zu	to

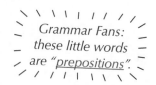

Grammar Fans: these little words are "<u>prepositions</u>".

These are the datives for **der**, **ein**, **mein** and **kein**

These are the datives for "<u>der</u>", "<u>ein</u>", "<u>mein</u>" and "<u>kein</u>". It's best to just <u>learn them</u>.

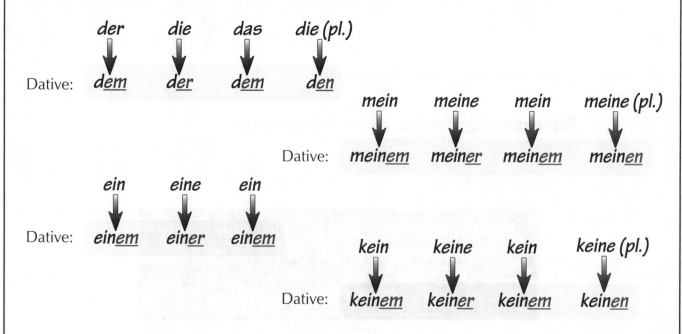

Learn these prepositions that take the dative case

You could make up a rhyme to help you remember these words. Something like... "in, von, auf, an, mit, gegenüber, zu take the dative case"... or maybe something a bit more catchy.

The Dative Case

Once you've learnt <u>when</u> you need to use the dative (see previous page),
you need to learn <u>how</u> to use it. That's what this page is all about...

This is **how** you use the **dative**

Say you've got to write "<u>We're playing with my brother</u>" — in German...

1) Write your sentence as far as "<u>mit</u>":

Wir spielen mit ➡ *mein<u>em</u> Bruder*

2) Now get the right, <u>dative</u> bit, of "<u>mein</u>". "<u>Bruder</u>" is a masculine word — so it's "<u>meinem</u>" (see previous page).

3) Put it all together and you get the sentence:

Wir spielen mit mein<u>em</u> Bruder. = We're playing with my brother.

Here are some more examples of the dative in action:

Das Kino ist gegenüber <u>der</u> Backerei. = The cinema is opposite the bakery.

Er liest eine Postkarte von ein<u>er</u> Freundin. = He reads a postcard from a friend.

You have to make dative plural <u>nouns</u> end in "n" too:

mit mein<u>en</u> Hunde<u>n</u> = with my dogs (dat.)

"**Dem**" and "**der**" **change** some prepositions

Some prepositions get <u>shortened</u> when you use them with "<u>dem</u>" or "<u>der</u>".

in + dem = im
von + dem = vom
an + dem = am
zu + der = zur *zu + dem = zum*

Examples:

in dem Bett ➡ *<u>im</u> Bett* = in the bed

Instead of saying "in dem" you join them together and say "im".

zu der Kirche ➡ *<u>zur</u> Kirche* = to the church

Instead of saying "zu der" you join them together and say "zur".

Practice Questions

1   Write out the accusative (object) form of these words by putting "den", "die" or "das" in front of them. I've done the first one for you.

a) *den* Wagen [der]

b) .... Getränk [das]

c) .... Schwester [die]

d) .... Monat [der]

e) .... Maus [die]

f) .... Jahr [das]

g) .... Speisekarte [die]

h) .... Schloss [das]

i) .... Blumenkohl [der]

2   Write out the accusative (object) form of these words by putting the correct form of "ein", "mein" or "kein" in front of them. I've done three examples for you.

EIN/EINE

a) *einen* Handschuh [der]

b) .... Eis [das]

c) .... Keks [der]

d) .... Bluse [die]

MEIN/MEINE

e) *mein* Frühstück [das]

f) .... Adresse [die]

g) .... Bruder [der]

h) .... Orange [die]

KEIN/KEINE

i) *keine* Banane [die]

j) .... Steak [das]

k) .... Brille [die]

l) .... Postkarte [die]

3   Write out the dative form of these words by putting the correct form of "ein", "mein" or "kein" in front of them. I've done three examples for you.

EIN/EINE

a) *einem* Pfirsich [der]

b) .... Erdbeere [die]

c) .... Wagen [der]

d) .... Speisekarte [die]

MEIN/MEINE

e) *meiner* Maus [die]

f) .... Hemd [das]

g) .... Hund [der]

h) .... Karte [die]

KEIN/KEINE

i) *keinem* Rotwein [der]

j) .... Theater [das]

k) .... Wurst [die]

l) .... Joghurt [der]

4   Copy and complete these sentences using the preposition in capitals and the correct dative form of "der", "die" or "das". I've done the first one for you.

a) *IN*: Ich wohne .... Stadt. [die]   *Ich wohne in der Stadt.*

b) *ZU*: Frau Weber geht .... Bäckerei. [die]

c) *AUF*: Der Kaffee ist .... Tisch. [der]

d) *ZU*: Wir fahren .... Schloss. [das]

e) *GEGENÜBER*: Die Bibliothek ist .... Post. [die]

f) *VON*: Der Brief ist .... Frau. [die]

g) *IN*: Ist sie .... Kino? [das]

Adjectives — Words to Describe Things

Adjectives are words that <u>describe things</u>, like "green", "massive" and "slimy". You sometimes <u>change the endings</u> in German — it depends what word comes <u>before</u> the adjective.

The dress IS big — adjectives don't change after 'is'

This is the <u>easiest</u> way to use adjectives.
With sentences like this, you stick the adjective in <u>just as it is</u>.

Mein Kleid ist groß.

= My dress is <u>big</u>.

black: schwarz
old: alt

You can use this type of sentence to give opinions too — see p.100.

THE big dress — after der, die and das, ADD E

When the adjective comes after "<u>der</u>", "<u>die</u>" or
"<u>das</u>", you stick an "<u>e</u>" on the end of the adjective.

der, die, das ➞ *große*

der große Pulli

= the big pullover

die große Jacke

= the big jacket

das große Kleid

= the big dress

The adjective goes <u>between</u> the "<u>der</u>", "<u>die</u>" or "<u>das</u>" and the word you're describing.

A big dress — after ein, the endings are different

Add these endings to the adjective if it comes after "<u>ein</u>", "<u>eine</u>" and "<u>ein</u>".

ein ➞ *blauer*

This is what you use with <u>masculine</u> words.

eine ➞ *blaue*

This is what you use with <u>feminine</u> words.

ein ➞ *blaues*

This is what you use with <u>neuter</u> words.

EXAMPLES: **ein blauer Pulli**

= a blue pullover

eine blaue Jacke

= a blue jacket

ein blaues Kleid

= a blue dress

It's just like with "<u>der</u>", "<u>die</u>" and "<u>das</u>" — the adjective goes <u>after</u> the "<u>ein</u>" or "<u>eine</u>", and <u>before</u> the thing you're <u>describing</u>.

Make sure you know your adjective endings
After "der", "die" and "das" it's pretty straightforward — you just add "e". It gets a bit more complicated with "ein", "eine" and "ein" though. Oh well. You'll just have to learn them.

Making Comparisons

Sometimes you don't just want to say that something is big, or red or whatever.
You might want to say that something is <u>bigger than</u> or <u>more red</u> than something else.

My dress is cheaper — add **ER** to the adjective

If you need to say something is <u>faster</u>, <u>slower</u>, <u>more grungy</u>, or whatever,
take the basic adjective and add "<u>er</u>":

*Grammar Fans:
these are called
"<u>comparatives</u>".*

billig + <u>*er*</u> ➡ *billig<u>er</u>*

= cheap + <u>er</u>   = cheap<u>er</u>

Mein Kleid ist billiger.   = My dress is cheaper.

For some words you add an **umlaut** (¨) and **ER**

With a few words you don't <u>just</u> stick "<u>er</u>" on the end. You have to add an <u>umlaut</u> too.

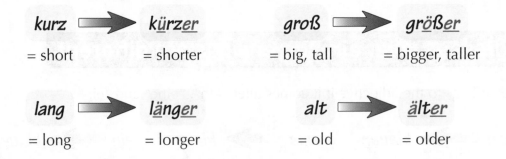

kurz ➡ *k<u>ü</u>rz<u>er</u>*   *groß* ➡ *gr<u>öß</u><u>er</u>*

= short   = shorter   = big, tall   = bigger, taller

lang ➡ *l<u>ä</u>ng<u>er</u>*   *alt* ➡ *<u>ä</u>lt<u>er</u>*

= long   = longer   = old   = older

The dictionary will say this:

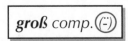

groß comp.(¨)

if you need an umlaut.

You can't just <u>guess</u> which words need an umlaut — learn them as you go along.

Add "er" to an adjective to make a comparison
Dictionaries really are marvellous. They tell you what a word is in German, what the plural is
(if it's a noun) and how to make it a comparison word — what more could you want...

Making Comparisons

When you compare things in English you use the word "than". The word for "than" in German is "als" and it gets used in a similar way. Read on to find out more...

Schöner als — nicer than

To compare <u>two</u> things, put "<u>als</u>" where you'd use "<u>than</u>" in English.

Deine Wohnung ist schöner <u>als</u> meine Wohnung.

= Your flat is nicer <u>than</u> my flat.

My tortoise is fastest — add -ste

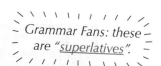
<u>Grammar Fans:</u> these are "<u>superlatives</u>".

The German way to say something is "<u>biggest</u>" or "<u>best</u>" is to add <u>-ste</u>.

schnell = fast ➡ **schnell<u>ste</u>** = fastest ➡ **der/die/das Schnell<u>ste</u>** = the fastest

E.g. **der schnellste Zug** = the fastest train

Er ist der Schnellste. = He is the fastest.

It can be a bit tricky depending on what letters come at the <u>end</u> of the word you're adding to:

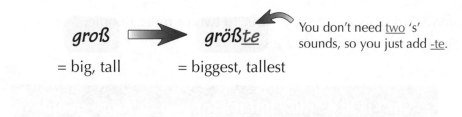

groß = big, tall ➡ **größ<u>te</u>** = biggest, tallest

You don't need <u>two</u> 's' sounds, so you just add <u>-te</u>.

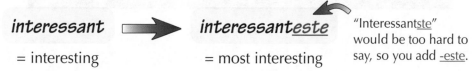

interessant = interesting ➡ **interessant<u>este</u>** = most interesting

"Interessant<u>ste</u>" would be too hard to say, so you add <u>-este</u>.

Add "ste" if you want to say something is the "most ...."

Most of the time, you just need to add "ste". If the word ends in "s" then you can just add "te". If you come across words that are exceptions to this rule, get them learnt.

Words for "You" — "du" and "ihr"

In German, there are <u>three words</u> that mean "<u>you</u>". They're "<u>du</u>", "<u>Sie</u>" and "<u>ihr</u>".
This page tells you <u>when</u> to use "<u>du</u>" and "<u>ihr</u>". Simple as that.

"du" is for a friend, a family member or a younger person

"du" is the informal, friendly way to say "you" to one person.
Technically, you'd say it's the "<u>informal singular</u>".

Use "du" for one person your age or younger

Use "du" for a friend or a close relative

Du bist sehr stark!

Use "du" for an animal or a pet

"ihr" is for two or more friends, family members, etc.

"ihr" is the informal friendly way to say "you" to two or more people.
Technically, you'd say it's the "<u>informal plural</u>".

"ihr" is like "du", but it's for two or more people

"Du" and "ihr" are for people you know well
You can use "du" and "ihr" if you're talking to friends and family, or someone your own age.
If you're talking to an adult you don't know, you should use "Sie" (which is on the next page).

Words for "You" — "Sie"

"Sie" is the third way of saying "you". You use it when you want to be polite.

Use "Sie" for older people and to be polite

"Sie" is the formal way to say "you". It's the same for one, two or more people.
Technically, you'd say it's the "formal singular or plural".

> **Use "Sie" to be polite to older people**
> **(who aren't close family or friends)**

Examples — when to use the different words for "you"

Here's how you'd ask a selection of different people how old they are:

1) Your dad: *Wie alt bist <u>du</u>?*   = How old are <u>you</u>?

2) A German kid you've just met: *Wie alt bist <u>du</u>?*   = How old are <u>you</u>?

3) Your dog: *Wie alt bist <u>du</u>?*   = How old are <u>you</u>?

4) Two friends: *Wie alt seid <u>ihr</u>?*   = How old are <u>you</u>?

5) The Queen: *Wie alt sind <u>Sie</u>?*   = How old are <u>you</u>?

If you're still having trouble, try learning this <u>flow chart</u>:

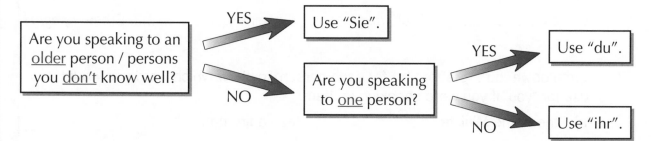

"Sie" — it's easier than it looks

You might not think you'd use "Sie" very much. But if you went to Germany you'd use it quite a bit — e.g. talking to shop assistants or asking for directions, so you need to know how it works.

Practice Questions

<u>Listening Questions</u>

Listen to these three people talking about their friends.
Write down whether each of these sentences is true or false.

1   Carola is smaller than Bernd.

2   a)   Katja is the tallest in her family.

   b)   Katja has three older brothers.

3   a)   Sonja has longer hair than Andrea.

   b)   Andrea has a bigger flat than Sonja.

4   Copy and complete these sentences, using the words from the box below
   to fill in the blanks. The bits in brackets tell you what they should say.

   a)   Mein Hemd ist .... *(My shirt is <u>yellow</u>.)*

   b)   Der Rock ist .... *(The skirt is <u>big</u>.)*

   c)   Die Jacken sind .... *(The jackets are <u>old</u>.)*

   d)   Die Erbsen sind .... *(The peas are <u>green</u>.)*

grün	gelb
alt	groß

5   Copy and complete these phrases. This time they start with
   "der", "die" or "das". Look back at Q4 to help you.

   a)   das .... Hemd *(yellow)*   c)   die .... Jacke *(old)*

   b)   der .... Rock *(big)*   d)   die .... Erbse *(green)*

6   Copy and complete these phrases that start with "ein" or "eine".
   HINT: Watch out for the endings of the words you write in.

   a)   ein .... Hemd *(yellow)*   c)   eine .... Jacke *(old)*

   b)   ein .... Rock *(big)*   d)   eine .... Erbse *(green)*

7   Write down "du", "Sie" or "ihr" for each person, to show which word you would
   use for "you" if you were speaking to them.

   a)   the Prime Minister   e)   a fireman

   b)   a classmate   f)   your parents

   c)   your sister   g)   your cat

   d)   the Queen   h)   a teacher in school

Verbs — Present Tense

You need to know what a verb <u>is</u> to understand this page. Verbs are "<u>doing</u>" or "<u>being</u>" words.

Verbs are **action words** — they tell you what's going on

She <u>eats</u> rice for lunch.

"<u>doing</u>" words

Joe <u>rides</u> to Tibet every day.

I <u>am</u> very happy.

"<u>being</u>" words

Today <u>is</u> a good day.

The **present** tense is what's happening **now**

1) When you look verbs up in a <u>dictionary</u>, it'll give you the "<u>infinitive</u>" form.
    For example, "machen" = "to do", "kaufen" = "to buy".

2) To say something in the <u>present tense</u>, you need to <u>change</u> the verb.
    For regular verbs take the <u>front part</u> of the verb (without the "<u>en</u>"), and stick on an <u>ending</u>.

3) The <u>endings are the same</u> for all <u>regular verbs</u>.
    "<u>Machen</u>" is regular, so here it is with its endings...

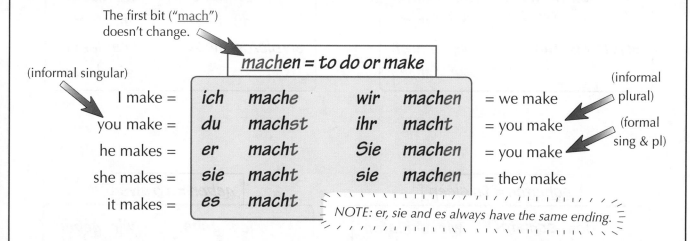

The first bit ("<u>mach</u>")
doesn't change.

__machen = to do or make__

(informal singular)

I make =	ich	mache	wir	machen	= we make
you make =	du	machst	ihr	macht	= you make
he makes =	er	macht	Sie	machen	= you make
she makes =	sie	macht	sie	machen	= they make
it makes =	es	macht			

(informal plural)

(formal sing & pl)

NOTE: er, sie and es always have the same ending.

For example, if you want to say something like "He <u>buys</u> bread", it's dead easy:

Start by <u>knocking off</u> the "<u>en</u>".

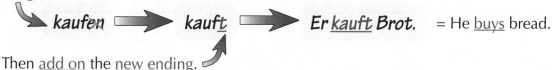

kaufen ➡ **kau<u>ft</u>** ➡ **Er <u>kauft</u> Brot.**   = He <u>buys</u> bread.

Then <u>add on</u> the <u>new ending</u>.

Here are some more <u>regular verbs</u> — i.e. these
verbs all follow the same pattern as "<u>machen</u>".
Learn the endings for one and you've learnt them all.

to ask:	fragen
to play:	spielen
to buy:	kaufen

Verbs — Present Tense

Some verbs have different endings to the ones on p.123. You need to learn these awkward verbs so you can use them correctly. Here's a lovely page all about them...

Learn these awkward verbs

These verbs <u>don't</u> follow the pattern of regular verbs in the present tense — they have weird "<u>du</u>" and "<u>er/sie/es</u>" forms.

<u>ess</u>en = to eat

ich esse	wir essen
du isst	ihr esst
er/sie/es isst	Sie essen
	sie essen

<u>seh</u>en = to see

ich sehe	wir sehen
du siehst	ihr seht
er/sie/es sieht	Sie sehen
	sie sehen

<u>fahr</u>en = to go / drive

ich fahre	wir fahren
du fährst	ihr fahrt
er/sie/es fährt	Sie fahren
	sie fahren

<u>les</u>en = to read

ich lese	wir lesen
du liest	ihr lest
er/sie/es liest	Sie lesen
	sie lesen

<u>schlaf</u>en = to sleep

ich schlafe	wir schlafen
du schläfst	ihr schlaft
er/sie/es schläft	Sie schlafen
	sie schlafen

<u>geb</u>en = to give

ich gebe	wir geben
du gibst	ihr gebt
er/sie/es gibt	Sie geben
	sie geben

It's the "du" and "er/sie/es" forms that break the rules

There's a lot of stuff on these pages and you need to learn it to be able to use verbs correctly. Make sure you know the rules for regular verbs and then learn all the exceptions too.

Sein and Haben

"Haben" and "sein" are the two German verbs you need the most.
They don't follow the normal pattern — you just have to learn them off by heart.

The present tense bits of **sein** and **haben** are **irregular**

① "sein" means "to be" — it's dead important, but it's also dead weird.

sein = to be

(informal singular)

I am =	ich	**bin**	wir	**sind**	= we are
you are =	du	**bist**	ihr	**seid**	= you are
he is =	er	**ist**	Sie	**sind**	= you are
she is =	sie	**ist**	sie	**sind**	= they are
it is =	es	**ist**			

(informal plural)

(formal sing & pl)

② "haben" means "to have" — it's the "hast" and "hat" bit that don't follow the pattern.

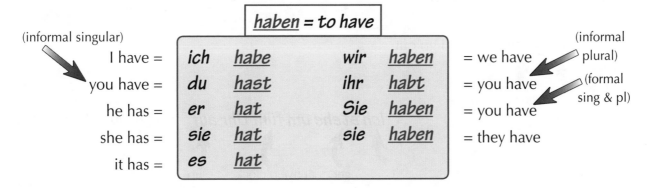

haben = to have

(informal singular)

I have =	ich	**habe**	wir	**haben**	= we have
you have =	du	**hast**	ihr	**habt**	= you have
he has =	er	**hat**	Sie	**haben**	= you have
she has =	sie	**hat**	sie	**haben**	= they have
it has =	es	**hat**			

(informal plural)

(formal sing & pl)

Ich habe den besten Hut.

Nein! Mein Hut ist sehr schick.

You have to learn the endings for "sein" and "haben"

"Sein" and "haben" are verbs you will use all the time. They're the most important verbs of all, so no excuses. You've just got to get your head down and learn them... right now.

Separable Verbs

Separable verbs can seem confusing, but they're <u>not</u> that hard really. Honest.

Separable verbs are made up of two bits

1) In <u>English</u>, there are loads of verbs made of <u>two bits</u>.
   For example, "go out" or "get up".

2) It's <u>similar</u> in <u>German</u>. What's tricky is knowing <u>where</u> the bits go.
   In the <u>infinitive</u> (see p.123), they're kind of <u>back-to-front</u>.

   EXAMPLES:

   ausgehen = to go out   ***aufstehen*** = to get up

   out   go   up   get

   When you use them in sentences like "I go out", you <u>split them up</u>,
   and put the <u>first</u> bit <u>right to the end of the sentence</u>.

   EXAMPLES:

   Ich gehe aus = I go out

   I   go   out

   Ich stehe um fünf Uhr auf = I get up at five o'clock

   I   get   at five o'clock   up

3) Here are the other separable verbs you need to know.
   The bit that breaks off is <u>underlined</u>.

to wash up:	<u>ab</u>waschen	*to arrive:*	<u>an</u>kommen
to watch TV:	<u>fern</u>sehen	*to leave:*	<u>ab</u>fahren
to phone/to ring up:	<u>an</u>rufen	*to seem:*	<u>aus</u>sehen

---

Think of the two bits as separate words

That box of separable verbs is there to be learnt, so don't turn over until you know them all.
Yep... that means knowing which bit breaks off and which bit stays put as well.

Modal Verbs

You use <u>modal verbs all the time</u> (even if you don't know you're doing it). They're all verbs you <u>use</u> in the <u>same kinda way</u> and they're all a bit <u>weird</u> — so you have to learn all the bits.

Modal verbs **change** what other verbs **mean**

Modal verbs are words like "can" and "must". They're called <u>MODAL</u> verbs because they <u>change</u> ("modify") the meaning of other verbs. Look at how <u>different</u> these sentences are, even though they're all to do with eating:

Ich kann essen.   *Ich will essen.*   *Ich soll essen.*

= I can eat.   = I want to eat.   = I should eat.

This is how you use them

You need the <u>right form</u> of the <u>modal verb</u> ("I want" or "he wants") because that's the main verb...

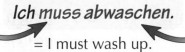

Ich muss abwaschen.

= I must wash up.

...and you need the <u>infinitive</u> of the <u>other verb</u> (the basic "en" form). You stick this at the <u>end of the sentence</u>.

Learn these **modal verbs**

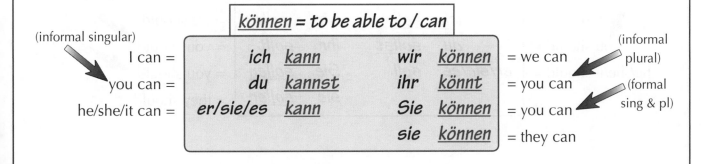

können = to be able to / can

(informal singular)

I can =	ich	kann	wir	können	= we can
you can =	du	kannst	ihr	könnt	= you can
he/she/it can =	er/sie/es	kann	Sie	können	= you can
			sie	können	= they can

(informal plural) (formal sing & pl)

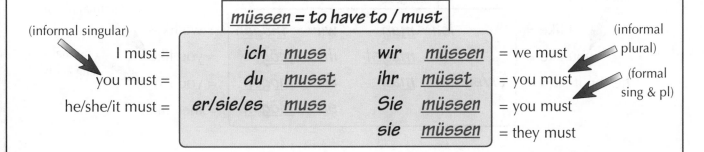

müssen = to have to / must

(informal singular)

I must =	ich	muss	wir	müssen	= we must
you must =	du	musst	ihr	müsst	= you must
he/she/it must =	er/sie/es	muss	Sie	müssen	= you must
			sie	müssen	= they must

(informal plural) (formal sing & pl)

Repeat after me — I must learn my modal verbs
Modal verbs are dead straightforward to put in a sentence — the only tricky bit is knowing which form of the verb to use. Which is why you really need to get learning those tables...

Modal Verbs

More modal verbs to learn

dürfen = to be allowed to (may)

(informal singular)

I'm allowed =	ich	darf	wir	dürfen	= we are allowed	(informal plural)
you are allowed =	du	darfst	ihr	dürft	= you are allowed	(formal sing & pl)
he/she/it is allowed =	er/sie/es	darf	Sie	dürfen	= you are allowed	
			sie	dürfen	= they are allowed	

wollen = to want

(informal singular)

I want =	ich	will	wir	wollen	= we want	(informal plural)
you want =	du	willst	ihr	wollt	= you want	(formal sing & pl)
he/she/it wants =	er/sie/es	will	Sie	wollen	= you want	
			sie	wollen	= they want	

sollen = to be supposed to / should

(informal singular)

I should =	ich	soll	wir	sollen	= we should	(informal plural)
you should =	du	sollst	ihr	sollt	= you should	(formal sing & pl)
he/she/it should =	er/sie/es	soll	Sie	sollen	= you should	
			sie	sollen	= they should	

mögen = to like

(informal singular)

I like =	ich	mag	wir	mögen	= we like	(informal plural)
you like =	du	magst	ihr	mögt	= you like	(formal sing & pl)
he/she/it likes =	er/sie/es	mag	Sie	mögen	= you like	
			sie	mögen	= they like	

Phew, I'm glad that's over...

Well it's not really over until you've learnt all these tables. I know it's a bit of a pain but there's no other way. Go through them one by one until you've got them all nailed.

Practice Questions

1 Copy and complete these sentences, by filling in the present tense form of the verb in brackets. They all follow the same pattern as "machen".

a) Ich .... (kaufen)

b) Ihr .... Deutsch. (verstehen)

c) Sie (you, formal) .... Pizza. (kaufen)

d) Du .... (fragen)

e) Wir .... Fußball. (spielen)

f) Er .... einen Fehler. (machen)

2 Copy and complete these lists with the correct form of each verb.
HINT: Watch out — these verbs don't follow the normal pattern.

a) <u>Essen</u>

ich ....

du isst

er ....

wir ....

ihr esst

Sie ....

b) <u>Fahren</u>

ich fahre

du ....

er fährt

wir ....

ihr ....

Sie fahren

c) <u>Schlafen</u>

ich schlafe

du ....

er ....

wir ....

ihr ....

Sie ....

3 Copy and complete these lists with the correct form of each verb.

a) <u>Sein</u>

ich bin

du ....

er/sie/es ....

wir ....

ihr ....

Sie ....

sie sind

b) <u>Haben</u>

ich ....

du hast

er/sie/es ....

wir haben

ihr ....

Sie ....

sie haben

4 Write these out in German. The verbs are all made up of two bits.

a) They get up. *Sie stehen auf.*

b) He goes out.

c) She rings up.

d) We leave.

e) They arrive.

f) We wash up.

5 Write these sentences out again, putting the words into the right order.

a) essen kann Peter

b) Sie Hunde mögen

c) soll schreiben ich

d) ich muss besuchen Tina

Commands and Orders

I command you to read this page, and learn all about telling people what to do in German.

Tell people what to do...

Grammar Fans: this is called the "imperative".

1) Giving people <u>orders</u> in German is pretty <u>straightforward</u>.

2) It's basically the <u>present tense</u> (see p.123), <u>fiddled about</u> a bit.

3) Just like the present tense, the <u>way</u> you say an order depends on <u>who you're talking to</u>. Look at this example for "Go!".

This is the important bit here.

HINTS:

Who you're talking to	Present tense	Imperative
one person, friendly	du gehst (you go)	Geh! (go!)
two or more, friendly	ihr geht (you go)	Geht! (go!)
any number, polite	Sie gehen (you go)	Gehen Sie! (go!)

Take off the "du" and the "st".

Take off the "ihr".

Put the "Sie" at the end.

See pages 120-121 for more on this stuff.

4) The key thing is those <u>hints</u> on the right-hand side. Take some time to <u>learn them</u>.

More examples:

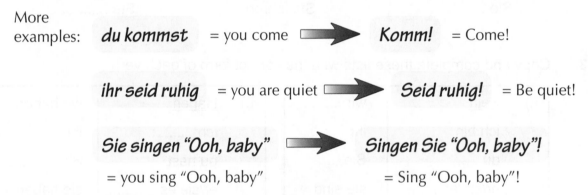

du kommst = you come ➡ *Komm!* = Come!

ihr seid ruhig = you are quiet ➡ *Seid ruhig!* = Be quiet!

Sie singen "Ooh, baby" ➡ *Singen Sie "Ooh, baby"!*

= you sing "Ooh, baby" = Sing "Ooh, baby"!

How to tell people what **NOT** to do

To tell people <u>not</u> to do something, just add "nicht" <u>after</u> the verb for <u>du</u> and <u>ihr</u>.

Geh <u>nicht</u>! = <u>Don't</u> go!   *Seid <u>nicht</u> ruhig!* = <u>Don't</u> be quiet!

For <u>Sie,</u> the "nicht" goes <u>straight after</u> the Sie.   *Gehen Sie <u>nicht</u>!* = <u>Don't</u> go!

See p.137 for more on "nicht".

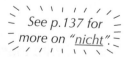

Learn!
It all boils down to those <u>3 hints</u>, and putting "<u>nicht</u>" on the <u>end</u> for <u>not</u>. Cover up the page, and write the hints down from <u>memory</u>. If you don't get them <u>100% right</u>, go over it and <u>try again</u>.

Talking About the Past

The past tense is mighty important. If you've ever been desperate to tell a German person what you had for tea last night but you weren't sure how to do it, these are the pages for you.

The **past tense** is for talking about the **past**...

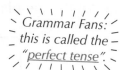

Here's how you make the past tense. There are <u>two</u> important bits.

Ich habe Fußball gespielt. = I (have) played football.

1) For most verbs, you start with the <u>present tense</u> of "<u>haben</u>" (see p.125).

2) This bit means "<u>played</u>". It's a <u>special version</u> of "spielen" (to play). This special past tense word <u>always</u> goes at the <u>end</u>.

You need to learn this **formula**

For all <u>regular</u> verbs, you use an easy formula to make the special past tense word.

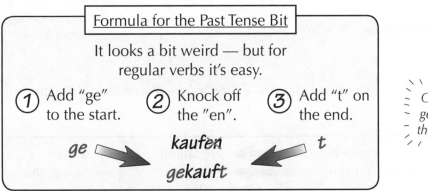

Formula for the Past Tense Bit

It looks a bit weird — but for regular verbs it's easy.

① Add "ge" to the start. ② Knock off the "en". ③ Add "t" on the end.

ge ⟶ *kaufen* ⟵ t

gekauft

Grammar Fans: the ge-blah bit is called the "<u>past participle</u>".

These regular verbs all follow the formula:

to play:	spielen	⟶	gespielt	:*played*
to buy:	kaufen	⟶	gekauft	:*bought*
to make / do:	machen	⟶	gemacht	:*made / done*
to ask:	fragen	⟶	gefragt	:*asked*
to say:	sagen	⟶	gesagt	:*said*
to hear:	hören	⟶	gehört	:*heard*

Here's another example: *Du hast ein Rad gekauft.* = <u>You have</u> bought a bicycle.

The ge-blah word goes at the end
Getting the word order right can be tricky. The present tense "haben" bit goes second and the special past tense word goes at the end. That's not it for the past tense though. Keep reading...

Talking About the Past

Some verbs **don't** follow the formula

Verbs that <u>don't</u> follow the formula on p.131 are called <u>irregular verbs</u>. For these you can't work out what the "ge-blah" word will be — you just have to <u>learn</u> them. Here are four important ones:

to eat:	essen	→	gegessen	*:eaten*
to write:	schreiben	→	geschr<u>ie</u>ben	*:written*
to see:	sehen	→	gesehen	*:seen*
to drink:	trinken	→	getrunken	*:drunk*

Some verbs need "**sein**" instead of "**haben**"

Some verbs need the <u>present tense</u> of "<u>sein</u>" rather than "haben" to make them <u>past tense</u>. It's kind of like saying "<u>I am gone</u>" instead of "<u>I have gone</u>".

<u>Ich bin</u> gegangen.   = I have gone / I went.

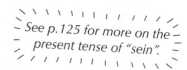

See p.125 for more on the present tense of "sein".

You'll need to learn which verbs need "I am" — they're usually ones to do with <u>movement</u>, e.g. to go, to run, to drive. All of these need "sein" instead of "haben".

to go:	gehen	→	gegangen	*:gone/went*
to go, drive:	fahren	→	gefahren	*:gone/went, driven/drove*
to fly:	fliegen	→	geflogen	*:flown/flew*
to run:	laufen	→	gelaufen	*:run/ran*
to come:	kommen	→	gekommen	*:come/came*

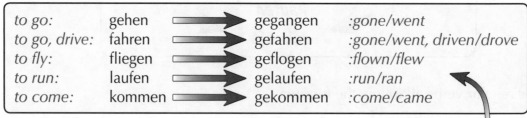

All of these are irregular, so you have to learn them off by heart.

Look at these examples:

<u>Sie ist</u> gelaufen.   = She has run / she ran.

<u>Wir sind</u> gefahren.   = We have driven / we drove.

Use the correct form of "haben" or "sein"

Remember: the "haben" or "sein" verb depends on who you're talking about. So you would say "Ich <u>bin</u>" but "Wir <u>sind</u>" — if you can't remember this stuff look back at page 125.

Talking About the Future

You use the <u>future tense</u> to talk about events that are <u>going to happen</u>... in the <u>future</u>.
There are <u>two ways</u> to form the future tense. We'll start with the <u>easy way</u>.

Talking about the future — the **easy** way

Pay attention and enjoy this — it's one of the few occasions I'll give you some really good news:

1) To say that something is <u>going to happen in the future</u>, you can just use the
   <u>normal present tense</u>, and <u>add a time phrase</u>.

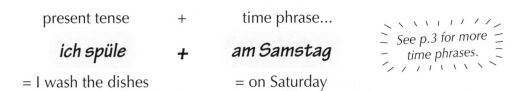

present tense	+	time phrase...
ich spüle	+	*am Samstag*
= I wash the dishes		= on Saturday

See p.3 for more time phrases.

...makes an easy sentence about the future:

=   *Ich spüle am Samstag.*

= I'll wash the dishes on Saturday

2) The only tricky bit is <u>where</u> to put the <u>time phrase</u>.
   Stick it <u>after the verb</u> (the doing word — see p.123).

EXAMPLES:

Ich gehe am Dienstag ins Kino.

"Ich gehe" is the <u>verb</u> bit, so
"am Dienstag" goes <u>after it</u>.

= <u>I'm going</u> to the cinema <u>on Tuesday</u>.

Ich fliege nächstes Jahr nach Spanien.

= <u>I'm flying</u> to Spain <u>next year</u>.

I will wash the dishes next year

Wow, what a nice page that was. I bet you didn't think the future tense would be that easy.
There is another way to talk about the future in German, and it's covered on the next page...

Talking About the Future

Talking about the future — the **harder** way

Right, the harder way. This is real higher levels stuff. Only learn this after you've got the easy way (see previous page) completely sussed.

1) In <u>English</u>, you can make the <u>future tense</u> by using "<u>will</u>", and an <u>infinitive</u>. For example:

> ***He will sing.***

2) You can do the <u>same thing</u> in <u>German</u>. For example:

> ***Er wird singen.***   = He will sing.

3) The word for "will" <u>changes</u> to <u>match</u> the <u>person</u> you're talking about. You have to choose the right part of "<u>werden</u>". Look at these examples:

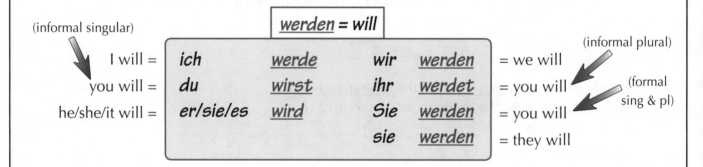

(informal singular)

<u>werden</u> = **will**			
I will =	*ich*	<u>werde</u>	*wir* <u>werden</u> = we will
you will =	*du*	<u>wirst</u>	*ihr* <u>werdet</u> = you will
he/she/it will =	*er/sie/es*	<u>wird</u>	*Sie* <u>werden</u> = you will
			sie <u>werden</u> = they will

(informal plural)

(formal sing & pl)

> ***Ich werde singen.***   = I will sing.   ***Wir werden singen.***   = We will sing.

4) One last thing — the <u>infinitive</u> (see p.123) always goes at the <u>end of the sentence</u>. Look at this example:

> ***Ich werde am Samstag singen.***   = I will sing on Saturday.

Show off by using "werden" to talk about the future

You'll need to show you can handle the future tense to gain the <u>higher levels</u>. Don't worry if you make the odd mistake. If you show that you've generally got the hang of it, you'll be fine.

Practice Questions

Listening Question

1 Listen to Bernard talking about his holidays and answer the questions in English.

a) Where did Bernard go on holiday last year?

b) What did his mum do?

c) What did he and his brother do?

d) Who is he going on holiday with next year?

e) What will they do?

f) Where will they stay?

2 Here are some things people have been told not to do.
Write down what they mean in English.

a) Singt nicht!

b) Lauf nicht!

c) Kommt nicht!

d) Sprechen Sie nicht!

e) Lesen Sie nicht!

f) Hör nicht zu!

g) Sitzt nicht!

3 Write the following out in German.
The bits in brackets tell you who you're talking to.

a) Sing! (ihr)

b) Don't speak! (Sie)

c) Be quiet! (ihr)

d) Sit! (ihr)

e) Go! (du)

f) Don't sing! (Sie)

g) Come! (du)

h) Don't go! (ihr)

Practice Questions

4   Change each verb into the past tense form (the past participle),
then write it out in English. I've done the first one for you.

a)   spielen (to play)   *gespielt (played)*

b)   fragen (to ask)

c)   hören (to listen)

d)   essen (to eat)

e)   trinken (to drink)

f)   schreiben (to write)

g)   sagen (to say)

h)   kaufen (to buy)

i)   machen (to make / do)

5   Here is a note of what Mark <u>has done</u> this morning. Write it out in German,
in full sentences. The verbs you need are all in Q4.

7.00	*I played football.*
8.30	*I ate.*
8.45	*I bought milk.*
9.30	*I wrote to Dieter.*
10.00	*I drank apple juice.*

HINTS:
football = Fußball
milk = Milch
to Dieter = an Dieter
apple juice = Apfelsaft

6   Rearrange these words to make proper sentences about the future.
The first one's been done for you.

a)   spüle Samstag am ich   *Ich spüle am Samstag.*

b)   fahre Jahr nach Spanien nächstes ich

c)   du hierhin nächste kommst Woche

d)   machst Montag am du das

7   Write these sentences out in German.

a)   I will sing on Saturday.

b)   He will visit tomorrow.

c)   She will go to Spain next week.

d)   I will go to Portugal next year.

e)   I will clean tomorrow.

f)   They will sleep tomorrow.

HINT: to visit = besuchen
to clean = putzen

Negatives — Nicht

Normally, people'll tell you "ahh, don't be so negative". Not this time, pal. Useful stuff, <u>read on</u>.

With a verb, you use "**nicht**" to say "**not**"

1) In <u>English</u> you change a sentence to mean the opposite by adding "<u>not</u>".

> EXAMPLE: *I am sporty.*   *I am <u>not</u> sporty.*

2) You can do the <u>same</u> in <u>German</u> — just add "nicht".

> EXAMPLE: *Ich bin sportlich.*   *Ich bin <u>nicht</u> sportlich.*
>
>   = I am sporty.   = I am <u>not</u> sporty.

Examples

Ich lese.   = I read.

              Ich lese <u>nicht</u>.   = I <u>don't</u> read.

Ich liebe dich.   = I love you.

              Ich liebe dich <u>nicht</u>.   = I <u>don't</u> love you.

Use "nicht" with verbs

Using "nicht" might seem simple, but it's easy to get it mixed up with "kein" (see the next page). Just remember that if the "not" goes with the verb, then you always use "nicht".

Negatives — Kein

With a noun, you use "**kein**" to say "**not**"

1) In <u>English</u>, you <u>can</u> add "<u>no</u>" to make a sentence negative, as in this popular song
(all together now...)

EXAMPLE:

We have bananas. ➡ *We have <u>no</u> bananas.*

2) It sometimes sounds <u>odd</u> in <u>English</u>, but it's <u>normal in German</u>.
You use "<u>kein</u>" before a noun — it means "no" / "not any".

"<u>Bananen</u>" is the <u>noun</u>.
The "<u>kein</u>" goes <u>before</u> it.

EXAMPLE:

Wir haben Bananen. ➡ *Wir haben <u>keine</u> Bananen.*

= We have bananas. = We have not (haven't) any bananas.

3) "<u>kein</u>" follows the same rules for <u>endings</u> as "<u>ein</u>".
For most sentences like this, you need the <u>accusative endings</u>:

Accusative Endings for Kein			
masculine singular	*feminine singular*	*neuter singular*	*plural (masculine, feminine or neuter)*
keinen	*keine*	*kein*	*keine*

Don't use "**nicht**" when you should use "**kein**"

The tricky bit is <u>when</u> to use "<u>kein</u>" and "<u>nicht</u>" (see previous page). Remember that "<u>nicht</u>"
means "<u>not</u>", and "<u>kein</u>" means "<u>not any</u>". Try saying the sentence you're writing <u>in English</u>
with "<u>not any</u>" in it. If it <u>makes sense</u>, use <u>kein</u>; if it <u>doesn't</u>, use <u>nicht</u>.

EXAMPLE:

Ich bin <u>nicht</u> sportlich.   = I am not sporty.

This has to be <u>nicht</u>, because
"I am not any sporty" is rubbish.

Use "kein" when you mean "not any"
This is one of those <u>sneaky rules</u> that can be tricky to get your head around. But getting it right
will help you sound less like a beginner and more like an impressive <u>master of languages</u>.

Word Order

In German, words don't always come in the same <u>order</u> as you'd in English expect.

Simple sentences are just like English ones

For <u>simple sentences</u> like these ones you can translate <u>word-for-word</u> from English.

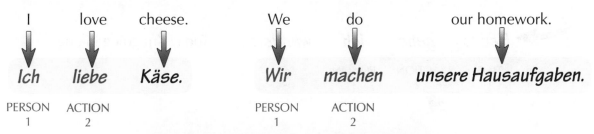

| I | love | cheese. | | We | do | our homework. |

Ich	**liebe**	**Käse.**		**Wir**	**machen**	**unsere Hausaufgaben.**
PERSON	ACTION			PERSON	ACTION	
1	2			1	2	

> **Start simple sentences with the PERSON, then the ACTION.**

You can join up simple sentences — just like in English

1) You can <u>join up</u> simple sentences with these words:

   UND = and   **ABER** = but   **ODER** = or

2) Here are two simple sentences with <u>normal</u> word order:

   Ich   bin   Berlinerin.   = I'm from Berlin.
   PERSON ACTION
      1   2

           Ich   esse   Currywurst nicht.   = I don't eat currywurst.
           PERSON ACTION
             1   2

3) Join them up using "<u>aber</u>" and you get:

   Ich bin Berlinerin <u>aber</u> ich esse Currywurst nicht.

   = I'm from Berlin <u>but</u> I don't eat Currywurst.

   Grammar Fans: these little words are called <u>conjunctions</u>.

4) The word order in each chunk of the new sentence stays <u>exactly the same</u> — brilliant.

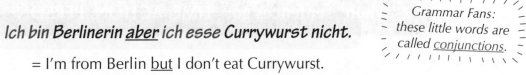

> **After "und", "aber" and "oder" the word order stays the SAME**

SECTION EIGHT — GRAMMAR AND PHRASES

Word Order

If you say WHEN the word order changes

1) In a sentence that says <u>when something happens</u>,
you can put the "when" word or time phrase <u>first</u>.

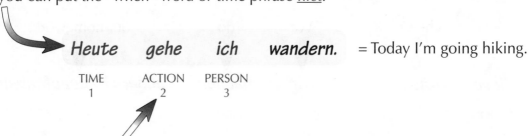

Heute   gehe   ich   wandern.   = Today I'm going hiking.

     TIME   ACTION   PERSON
     1   2   3

2) Then <u>swap</u> the action with the person, so the <u>action</u> comes second,
and the <u>person</u> comes third.

3) If there's a phrase with a <u>couple of words</u> for 'when', then the whole thing goes first.

EXAMPLES:

Nächste Woche   gehe   ich   schwimmen.   = Next week I'm going swimming.

     TIME   ACTION PERSON
     1   2   3

Am Montag   fährst   du   mit dem Bus.

     TIME   ACTION PERSON
     1   2   3

= On Monday you're going by bus.

"When" sentences go: TIME, ACTION, PERSON

The verb is usually the second bit in the sentence

Order word be can very confusing. Word be order can confusing. Aaaargh... I mean word order can be confusing. Learning the rules on these pages will help you work it out.

More on Word Order

This word order malarkey isn't over yet. This is where <u>joining words</u> (conjunctions) get <u>tricky</u>.

These words **change** the word order

These joining words change the word order in <u>two ways</u> — it all depends on <u>whether</u> they come in the <u>middle of a sentence</u> (see below) or <u>at the beginning</u> (see next page).

WEIL = because   **WENN** = if   **OBWOHL** = although

In the **MIDDLE** of a sentence...

> **When "WEIL", "WENN" and "OBWOHL" come in the middle of a sentence, shunt the VERB to the END.**

Example:

<u>Normally</u> "hat" goes here.   But after "<u>weil</u>" it goes <u>here</u>.

Suzi geht zum Arzt, weil sie Kopfschmerzen <u>hat</u>.

= Suzi goes to the doctor's, because she a headache <u>has</u>.

Here's another one:

<u>Normally</u> "ist" goes here.   But after <u>obwohl</u> it goes <u>here</u>.

Vati spielt Golf, obwohl es neblig <u>ist</u>.

= Father plays golf, although it foggy <u>is</u>.

Wo ist meine Kugel?

"Weil", "wenn" and "obwohl" send the verb to the end

The only way to get this right is to learn the words that mess up the word order. Try saying "I go swimming, because it is fun" in German and see if you can put the verb in the right place.

More on Word Order

At the BEGINNING of a sentence...

When "weil", "wenn" and "obwohl" come at the beginning of a sentence they make things seriously tricky. Take this slowly.

Wenn es kalt ist, komme ich mit dem Bus.

= If it's cold, I come by bus.

1) "Wenn" bumps the verb to the end of this bit of the sentence:

Wenn es kalt ist,

2) In the next bit of the sentence you swap the ACTION and the PERSON.

Normally it's...

ich komme

...but after "wenn" you put...

komme ich mit dem Bus.

> **If "WENN", "WEIL" or "OBWOHL" comes
> at the beginning of a sentence you get
> ACTION-COMMA-ACTION**

Wenn es kalt ist, komme ich mit dem Bus.

Action-Comma-Action is the secret to word-order success

In sentences like this, which start with "wenn", "weil" or "obwohl" and have a comma in the middle, you want to end up with the verbs (action words) either side of the comma. Try it out.

Important Tables

There's <u>nothing new</u> on this page — if you've read the rest of the book you've seen it all before. It's all a bit boring, but it's <u>so important</u> I've put it in <u>twice</u>.

You've got to know the **past**, **present** and **future**

1) "Normal" present tense:

machen = *to do, make*	
I do	*ich mach<u>e</u>*
you do	*du mach<u>st</u>*
he/she/it does	*er/sie/es mach<u>t</u>*
we do	*wir mach<u>en</u>*
you do	*ihr mach<u>t</u>*
you do	*Sie mach<u>en</u>*
they do	*sie mach<u>en</u>*

singular, informal

plural, informal

sing. & pl., formal

2) "Normal" past tense:

machen = *to do, make*	
I did	*ich <u>habe</u> gemacht*
you did	*du <u>hast</u> gemacht*
he/she/it did	*er/sie/es <u>hat</u> gemacht*
we did	*wir <u>haben</u> gemacht*
you did	*ihr <u>habt</u> gemacht*
you did	*Sie <u>haben</u> gemacht*
they did	*sie <u>haben</u> gemacht*

singular, informal

plural, informal

sing. & pl., formal

<u>Machen</u> is a 'normal' regular verb. There are lots of exceptions. Learn them as you go along.

3) "Normal" future tense:

machen = *to do, make*	
I will do	*ich <u>werde</u> machen*
you will do	*du <u>wirst</u> machen*
he/she/it will do	*er/sie/es <u>wird</u> machen*
we will do	*wir <u>werden</u> machen*
you will do	*ihr <u>werdet</u> machen*
you will do	*Sie <u>werden</u> machen*
they will do	*sie <u>werden</u> machen*

singular, informal

plural, informal

sing. & pl., formal

<u>Sein</u> is the weirdest of weird verbs:

sein = *to be, present tense*	
I am	*ich <u>bin</u>*
you are	*du <u>bist</u>*
he/she/it is	*er/sie/es <u>ist</u>*
we are	*wir <u>sind</u>*
you are	*ihr <u>seid</u>*
you are	*Sie <u>sind</u>*
they are	*sie <u>sind</u>*

singular, informal

plural, informal

sing. & pl., formal

Learn these tables

Crikey. That page certainly wasn't a bundle of laughs. You might have learnt these tables the first time they came up, but if not, take the time to learn them now. Go on, I dare you.

Important Tables

These words are little but dead **important**

THE — the definite article

	MASCULINE	FEMININE	NEUTER	PLURAL
NOMINATIVE (normal)	der	die	das	die
ACCUSATIVE (see p.112)	den	die	das	die
DATIVE (see p.114)	dem	der	dem	den

A — the indefinite article

	MASCULINE	FEMININE	NEUTER
NOMINATIVE (normal)	ein	eine	ein
ACCUSATIVE (see p.112)	einen	eine	ein
DATIVE (see p.114)	einem	einer	einem

MY, YOUR, HIS, THEIR — the possessive adjectives

singular, informal

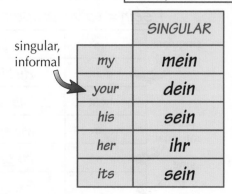

	SINGULAR
my	mein
your	dein
his	sein
her	ihr
its	sein

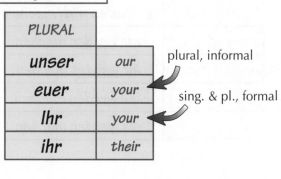

plural, informal

sing. & pl., formal

	PLURAL	
unser	our
euer	your
Ihr	your
ihr	their

The possessive adjectives and kein use exactly the same endings as ein.
(Apart from the plurals, which go NOM: keine, ACC: keine, DAT: keinen.)

Yippeee, the end of the grammar section — gold stars all round

Don't even try and learn everything on these pages in one go. If you do you'll probably make your ears bleed. Get one bit at a time soaked into your brain before you go on to the next.

Practice Questions

1   Write the following sentences in the negative form.
Then say what they mean in English. I've done the first one for you.

    a)   Wir haben Bananen. (We have bananas.)   *Wir haben keine Bananen.*
                                                              (We have no bananas.)

    b)   Die Lampe ist rot. (The lamp is red.)

    c)   Ich habe einen Bruder.   (I have a brother.)

    d)   Sie ist meine Mutter. (She is my mother.)

    e)   Bettina isst einen Apfel. (Bettina eats an apple.)

2   Rearrange these words to make proper sentences. Think about the word order.

    a)   Hunger ich habe   d)   Kino ich ins gehe samstags

    b)   Fußball ich morgen spiele   e)   ich Tee trinke

    c)   du kein heute hast Essen   f)   Berlinerin sie ist

3   Copy and complete these sentences using the German for the joining word shown.

    a)   Heute habe ich Hunger .... ich habe nichts zum Essen. **AND**

    b)   Ich spiele Fußball .... Klavier. **AND**

    c)   Du fährst mit dem Bus .... ich gehe ins Kino. **BUT**

    d)   Ich esse Pizza .... Currywurst. **OR**

    e)   Sie sprechen Deutsch .... sie wohnen hier. **BUT**

4   Match the German words on the left with their English meaning on the right.

    1. weil   a. although

    2. wenn   b. because

    3. obwohl   c. if

5   Join these phrases together, and write them out as **one sentence**, using the German for the joining word shown. I've done the first one for you.
HINT: Watch out for the word order.

    a)   Ich spiele Fußball. + **IF** + Ich habe Zeit.
         (I play football. + IF + I have time.)   *Ich spiele Fußball, wenn ich Zeit habe.*

    b)   Ich koche nicht gern. + **ALTHOUGH** + Essen ist toll.
         (I hate cooking. + ALTHOUGH + Food is terrific.)

    c)   Ich habe Hunger. + **BECAUSE** + Ich habe heute morgen Fußball gespielt.
         (I am hungry. + BECAUSE + I played football this morning.)

    d)   **ALTHOUGH** + Es ist neblig. + Meine Mutter spielt Fußball.
         (ALTHOUGH + It's foggy. + My mother is playing football.)

SECTION EIGHT — GRAMMAR AND PHRASES

Practice Questions

6   Copy and complete the missing bits of these lists.

PRESENT tense — spielen [to play]

ich spiele

du ....

er / sie / es ....

wir ....

ihr ....

Sie spielen

sie ....

PAST tense — kaufen [to buy]

ich ....

du hast gekauft

er / sie / es ....

wir ....

ihr habt gekauft

Sie ....

sie ....

FUTURE tense — schwimmen [to swim]

ich ....

du ....

er / sie / es wird schwimmen

wir werden schwimmen

ihr ....

Sie ....

sie ....

PAST tense — fahren [to go]

ich ....

du bist gefahren

er / sie / es ....

wir ....

ihr seid gefahren

Sie ....

sie ....

7   The fun's almost over. Copy and complete these tables.

The Definite Article — der, die, das

	masculine	feminine	neuter	plural
Nominative	....	die	....	die
Accusative	den	....	....	....
Dative	....	....	dem	....

KEIN, KEINE, KEIN

	masculine	feminine	neuter	plural
Nominative	....	keine	....	....
Accusative	....	....	....	....
Dative	keinem	....	keinem	....

Summary Questions

I admit it — that <u>was</u> the nastiest of nasty sections in this book. But it wouldn't achieve the full bloom of nastiness without some nasty summary questions to top it all off. You know how it works after me banging on for 146 pages — keep at it till you can answer <u>all</u> the questions <u>without</u> looking back. Only then can you be sure you <u>know your stuff</u>.

1) Translate these sentences into German:
   a) I like cake. b) I love cake. c) I like eating cake. d) Cake is totally brilliant.

2) Write these questions out in German: a) Do you like cats? b) Do you eat cats?
   c) When do you eat cats? d) Why do you eat cats?
   (Katzen = cats; you like = du magst; you eat = du isst)

3) Write all these words out, and give the nouns a capital letter at the beginning:
   tisch   wagen   sein   der   jacke   wenn   haus   hunger   fußball   tragen

4) Are these masculine, feminine, or neuter? a) der Tisch   b) die Küche   c) das Sofa

5) Write all these out in German (violin = die Geige): a) a violin b) my violin c) his violin
   d) their violin   e) your violin (informal, singular) f) your violin (informal, plural)

6) Rewrite these sentences, with er, sie, es or wir instead of the names of the people or things.
   a) Liese, Lotte und ich reden. b) Die Katze isst.   c) Anton spielt Klavier.

7) Fill the gaps in these sentences with der, die, das or den.
   a) _____ schnellste Pferd hat gewonnen. b) Der Vogel kauft _____ Pferd.
   c) Das Pferd liebt _____ Vogel. d) _____ Katze hasst _____ Mäuse.

8) Use each of these words once to fill in the gaps: eine   mein   keinen
   a) My car goes slowly. _____ Wagen fährt langsam.
   b) Have you got a guitar? Haben Sie _____ Gitarre?
   c) I haven't got a cauliflower today. Heute habe ich _____ Blumenkohl.

9) Choose the right word to fill the gap in each sentence.
   a) der / die / das / dem   Ich sitze auf _____ Tisch.
   b) ein / eine / einem   Ich wohne gegenüber _____ Park.
   c) mein / meine / meiner   Du spielst mit _____ Schwester.

10) Translate these phrases into German: a) the big rabbit b) a small dog c) a small cat

11) Translate these into German:
    a) The rabbit is bigger. b) The rabbit is bigger than the dog.
    c) The cat is smaller than the dog. d) The rabbit is the biggest.

12) To say "you" to these people, would you say "du", "Sie" or "ihr"?
    a) your mum b) your mate's annoying little brother
    c) everyone else in your class d) your head teacher (to his/her face)

13) Translate these into German: a) he is drinking (trinken)   b) we have (haben)
    b) you (singular, informal) are reading (lesen)   d) they are (sein)

14) Translate these into German: a) He phones at four o'clock. b) Today I am washing up.

15) (For a change) stick these into German: a) I should go. b) She likes cheese.

16) What do these mean in English? a) Schwimm! b) Essen Sie! c) Sprich!

17) Put the missing bit of haben in to make these sentences past tense, and translate them:
    a) Ich _____ eine Postkarte geschrieben.   b) Wir _____ den Vogel gehört.
    c) Ihr _____ zwanzig Fragen gefragt.

18) Put the missing bit of werden in to make these sentences future tense, and translate them:
    a) Du _____ spielen. b) Sie (she) _____ essen. c) Ihr _____ sehen.

Answers

Page 5

1) a) clock 4   d) clock 1
   b) clock 2   e) clock 6
   c) clock 3   f) clock 5

2) a) 73   f) 86
   b) 92   g) 3
   c) 12   h) 10
   d) 31   i) 5
   e) 25   j) 16

3) a) tomorrow   d) month
   b) week   e) afternoon
   c) evening   f) day

4) b) am sechzehnten April
   c) am ersten Juli
   d) am achtundzwanzigsten Februar
   e) am dritten September
   f) am neunundzwanzigsten Mai

Pages 11-12

1) a) False   c) False
   b) False   d) True

2) b) guten Abend
   c) gute Nacht
   d) guten Morgen
   e) hallo
   f) guten Tag
   g) auf Wiedersehen
   h) tschüss

3) 1c (Darf ich Ihnen Bernd vorstellen?)
   2d (Darf ich Ihnen meine Freundin vorstellen?)
   3b (Darf ich euch Bernd vorstellen?)
   4a (Darf ich dir Bernd vorstellen?)

4) a) danke   d) geht
   b) dir   e) schön
   c) geht's

5) a) I want   d) May I
   b) please   e) thank you very much
   c) I would like   f) you're welcome

6) b) Ich möchte hier sitzen.
   c) Ich möchte ein Brötchen.
   d) Ich möchte spülen.

Pages 20-21

1) a) 5 (Wilhelm, his brother, his stepmother, his father and his grandmother)
   b) Wilhelm's grandmother's cat
   c) Green
   d) (quite/fairly/rather) lazy

2) 1d (Ich habe am dritten Mai Geburtstag. = My birthday is on the 3rd of May.)
   2h (Was magst du? = What do you like?)
   3b (Ich heiße Aleesha. = I'm called Aleesha.)
   4f (Ich bin neunzehn Jahre alt. = I am nineteen.)
   5c (Wie heißt du? = What are you called?)
   6a (Ich mag Fußball. = I like football.)
   7g (Wie alt bist du? = How old are you?)
   8e (Wann hast du Geburtstag? = When is your birthday?)

3) a) False   d) True
   b) False   e) False
   c) True   f) True

4) meine Großmutter = Maria; mein Großvater = Peter;
   meine Tante = Lisa; mein Onkel = Bob; mein Cousin = Roger;
   meine Cousine = Sophie; mein Bruder = Phil.

5) a) der Vogel
   b) der Hund
   c) das Kaninchen
   d) die Kuh
   e) der Hamster
   f) die Schildkröte

6) b) Ich habe ein Kaninchen.
   c) Sie hat einen Hamster.
   d) Du hast eine Katze.
   e) Mein Hund ist böse.
   f) Meine Schildkröte heißt "Speedy".

Pages 28-29

1) a) 4
   b) 3
   c) 1
   d) 2

2) a) 6.30
   b) in the kitchen
   c) make her bed
   d) sets the table
   e) thinks it's boring

3) 1b (kitchen = die Küche)
   2f (dining room = das Esszimmer)
   3c (living room = das Wohnzimmer)
   4a (bedroom = das Schlafzimmer)
   5e (garden = der Garten)
   6d (bathroom = das Badezimmer)

4) a) ein
   b) Haus
   c) Zu .... Küche
   d) Was
   e) gibt
   f) es

5) a) I live in a big town/city.
   b) I live in a house.
   c) I live in the countryside.
   d) I live at the seaside.
   e) I live in a village.

6) a) Ich wasche mich.
   b) Ich sehe fern.
   c) Ich mache meine Hausaufgaben.
   d) Ich ziehe mich an.
   e) Ich gehe ins Bett.
   f) Ich gehe zur Schule.
   g) Ich stehe auf.
   h) Ich esse Frühstück.

7) b) Ich decke den Tisch.
   c) Ich mache mein Bett.
   d) Ich putze.
   e) Ich sauge Staub.
   f) Ich räume mein Zimmer auf.

Page 33

1) a) False
   b) True

2) a) True
   b) False

3) a) True
   b) True
4) a) das Auge   d) die Nase
   b) das Ohr   e) der Zahn (or die Zähne)
   c) die Haare   f) der Mund
5) a) das Knie   d) der Finger
   b) das Bein   e) der Bauch
   c) der Rücken   f) der Hals
6) 1e (pharmacy = die Apotheke)
   2a (hospital = das Krankenhaus)
   3b (I want to go to the doctor's = Ich will zum Arzt gehen)
   4d (doctor = der Arzt)
   5c (I am ill = Ich bin krank)
7) a) Ich habe Bauchschmerzen
   b) Meine Nase tut mir weh
   c) Ich habe Ohrenschmerzen
   d) Mein Bein tut mir weh
   e) Mein Rücken tut mir weh
   f) Ich habe Kopfschmerzen

Page 40

1) a) Positive
   b) No information
   c) Negative
2) a) Positive
   b) Positive
   c) Negative
3) a) Negative
   b) Positive
   c) No information
4) a) (die) Informatik   f) (die) Reli(gion)
   b) (die) Chemie   g) (der) Sport
   c) (die) Naturwissenschaft   h) (das) Französisch
   d) (die) Musik   i) (das) Spanisch
   e) (die) Biologie
5) a) Fahrrad   d) Fuß
   b) Stunden   e) Minuten
   c) fängt   f) stehe
6) a) timetable   d) ruler
   b) pen   e) exercise book
   c) rubber   f) book
7) a) Wie sagt man das auf Deutsch?
   b) Steht auf!
   c) richtig
   d) Was bedeutet das?
   e) Hört zu!
   f) die Lehrerin

Page 44

1) a) Physics
   b) His father
2) a) French
   b) Teacher or secretary
3) a) He thinks it's very interesting.
   b) Doctor or dentist
4)

Male	Female
Friseur	Bauarbeiterin
Büroangestellter	Krankenschwester
Schauspieler	Mechanikerin
Krankenpfleger	Polizistin
Arzt	Ingenieurin
Zahnarzt	Lehrerin

5) 1c (Ich bin Arzt = I am a doctor)
   2b (Mein Vater ist Mechaniker = My father is a mechanic)
   3d (Meine Mutter ist Verkäuferin = My mother is a salesperson)
   4a (Mein Freund George ist Ingenieur = My friend George is an engineer)
   5f (Ich arbeite bei Kwik Save = I work at Kwik Save)
   6e (Ich habe einen Teilzeitjob = I have a part-time job)

Page 50

1) a) 3
   b) 4
   c) 1
2) a) die Buchhandlung
   b) die Bäckerei
   c) die Apotheke
   d) die Metzgerei
   e) die Konditorei
3) 1g (das Kino = cinema)
   2f (das Verkehrsamt = tourist office)
   3d (die Bibliothek = library)
   4h (das Schloss = castle)
   5c (der Bahnhof = train station)
   6a (das Krankenhaus = hospital)
   7e (die Stadtmitte = town centre)
   8b (das Schwimmbad = swimming pool)

Pages 59-60

1) a) Onion soup, chicken and chips
   b) Pork with potatoes, cola
   c) Carrot soup, seafood pasta, white wine
2) a) das Lammfleisch
   b) die Meeresfrüchte
   c) das Schweinefleisch
   d) das Rindfleisch
   e) der Schinken
   f) das Hähnchen
3) (Supermarket:)   (Grocer's:)

(Supermarket:)	(Grocer's:)
a sausage	two lemons
fish	a pear
steak	an apple
mushrooms	an onion
a cauliflower	peas
four potatoes	three peaches
a cabbage	a banana
a lettuce	four oranges
five carrots	

4) a) 1. Kaffee
     2. Mineralwasser
     3. Orangensaft
     4. heiße Schokolade
     5. Cola
   b) Apfelsaft = apple juice
     Bier = beer
     Rotwein = red wine
     Weißwein = white wine
     Tee = tea
5) a) Hast du Durst? / Haben Sie Durst?
   b) Ich mag Schokolade nicht.
   c) Ich habe Hunger.
   d) Ich mag Marmelade nicht.
   e) Ich habe keinen Durst.
   f) Ich mag Milch.

6) a) At 7 o'clock.
   b) Cereal and coffee.
   c) She eats pork and rice, and drinks cola.
   d) At 1 o'clock.
   e) She eats chicken and pasta, and drinks white wine.

Page 65

1) a) Black trousers
   b) They're too big.
   c) A red hat
   d) €15,20

2) b) Mrs Becker wears a pink raincoat.
   c) Tobias wears green trousers.
   d) Anna wears a white skirt.
   e) My father wears a grey hat.
   f) He wears a red tie.

3) a) Sie trägt eine Baumwollbluse, einen blauen Rock, und schwarze Schuhe.
   b) Er trägt einen Wollpullover, und eine braune Hose.

4) a) Anything else?
   b) I'll leave it.
   c) How much is that?
   d) I'll take that one.
   e) It's 10 euros.

Page 72

1) a) True
   b) False
2) a) False
   b) True
3) a) False
   b) True
4) NB: You could put the instruments/sports in a different order.
   a) Ich spiele Kricket, Trompete und Schach.
   b) Ich spiele Klavier, Geige und Federball.
   c) Ich spiele Fußball und Tennis und ich spiele Schlagzeug.
   d) Ich spiele Klarinette, Schach und Tischtennis.
5) a) I listen to music.   c) I watch films.
   b) I read magazines.   d) I read novels.
6) b) Ich liebe Federball.
   c) Ich mag Schach nicht.
   d) Ich hasse Tennis.
7) b) , weil es einfach ist.
   c) , weil es langweilig ist.
   d) , weil es ermüdend ist.
   e) , weil es interessant ist.

Page 79 (tip box)

Fährt ein Zug nach München? Eine Rückfahrkarte, erste Klasse, bitte. Wann fährt der Zug?

Pages 80-81

1) a) 3
   b) 5
   c) 6
   d) 4
2) a) Single
   b) €20,90
   c) In 10 minutes
   d) Platform 7

3) b) das Freizeitzentrum
   c) das Kino
   d) das Schwimmbad
   e) das Restaurant
   f) das Theater
   g) zu Hause

4) You: Hast du Lust ins Kino zu gehen?
   You: Treffen wir uns um neunzehn Uhr.
   You: Treffen wir uns vor dem Verkehrsamt.

5) You: Was kostet eine Karte, bitte?
   You: Ich möchte vier Karten, bitte.
   You: Danke (schön).

6) a) coach   d) tram
   b) underground (train) e) train
   c) ship   f) bus

7)   Where   How
   a) Mainz   car
   b) Bonn   foot
   c) school   bicycle
   d) Italy   coach
   e) France   plane

Page 87

1) a) Hallo. Hier spricht .... Kann ich bitte mit Katharina sprechen?
   b) Wo ist sie, bitte?
   c) Meine Telefonnummer ist sechsundsiebzig, siebenunddreißig, fünfzehn. Danke, Frau Schulz.

2) a) Best wishes
   b) Write soon.
   c) Many thanks for your letter.
   d) See you soon.
   e) How are you?

3) a) Sam is a girl. (Lukas used "Liebe Sam", not "Lieber Sam".)
   b) I was very pleased to hear from you again.
   c) He says it's boring and difficult.
   d) Write soon.

4)   (your name and address)
      Großbritannien
      (your hometown), den (today's date in numbers separated by full stops)
      Sehr geehrter Herr Neumann,
      wenn möglich möchte ich bei Ihnen ein Doppelzimmer reservieren, vom 23. bis zum 28. Oktober. Könnten Sie mich bitte informieren, wie viel es kosten wird?
      Vielen Dank im Voraus. Mit freundlichen Grüßen,
      (your name)

Page 96-97

1)   France 4, 8
      Switzerland 3
      Belgium 2
      Holland 7
      Germany 1, 6
      Austria 5

2) a) True   d) True
   b) False   e) False
   c) False

3)   Normalerweise fahre ich nach Frankreich.
      Ich fahre mit meiner Tante.
      Ich übernachte in einer Jugendherberge.

4) b) Ein Einzelzimmer mit Toilette.
   c) Ein Einzelzimmer mit Dusche.
   d) Ein Doppelzimmer mit Bad.

5) b) youth hostel   e) sleeping bag
   c) pitch (space for a tent) f) drinking water
   d) caravan

a) Deutschland d) Großbritannien

b) Schottland e) das Vereinigte Königreich

c) Nordirland f) Frankreich

b) Ich bin Nordirländer. e) Ich bin Waliser.

c) Ich bin Irin. f) Ich bin Engländerin.

d) Ich bin Schottin.

age 103

a) Ich mag Tee. d) Ich hasse Goldfische.

b) Ich liebe Mathe. e) Ich mag Deutsch.

c) Ich mag Kaffee nicht. f) Ich mag Naturwissenschaften nicht.

) a) Geschichte ist toll.

b) Geschichte ist anstrengend.

c) Geschichte ist schwer.

d) Geschichte ist gut.

e) Geschichte ist fantastisch.

3) b) Heißt er Romeo?
(Is he called Romeo?)

c) Hast du einen Hund?
(Do you have a dog?)

d) Lernen wir Deutsch?
(Are we learning German?)

e) Gibt es hier in der Nähe ein Schloss?
(Is there a castle near here?)

4) 1e (Wann? = When?)

2b (Warum? = Why?)

3a (Was? = What?)

4g (Wer? = Who?)

5c (Wie? = How?)

6d (Wo? = Where?)

7f (Wohin? = Where (to)?)

Page 110-111

1) DER: Hund, Schuh, Kuli, Bruder, Onkel, Vater

DIE: Schwester, Katze, Freundin, Tante, Cousine

DAS Pferd, Knie, Haus, Ohr

2) 1e (Katze = Katzen)

2b (Hund = Hunde)

3f (Schuh = Schuhe)

4c (Banane = Bananen)

5h (Tante = Tanten)

6g (Freund = Freunde)

7a (Sofa = Sofas)

8d (Bett = Betten)

3) a) eine Katze f) ein Cousin

b) ein Hund g) ein Freund

c) ein Schuh h) ein Sofa

d) eine Banane i) ein Bett

e) eine Tante

4) a) mein Pferd i) mein Vater

b) mein Schuh j) meine Freundin

c) mein Kuli k) meine Tante

d) mein Hund l) mein Cousin

e) meine Katze m) mein Haus

f) mein Onkel n) mein Ohr

g) meine Schwester o) mein Knie

h) mein Bruder

5) a) mein Hund e) unser Cousin

b) ihr Bruder f) mein Pferd

c) mein Onkel g) sein Vater

d) ihre Freundin h) unsere Katze

6) b) Wir haben lange Haare. d) Sie kauft Brot.

c) Er ist hier. e) Wie alt ist er?

7) b) Er ist groß. c) Sie ist dumm. d) Er ist grün. e) Es ist schwarz.

Page 116

1) b) das Getränk f) das Jahr

c) die Schwester g) die Speisekarte

d) den Monat h) das Schloss

e) die Maus i) den Blumenkohl

2) b) ein Eis h) meine Orange

c) einen Keks j) kein Steak

d) eine Bluse k) keine Brille

f) meine Adresse l) keine Postkarte

g) meinen Bruder

3) b) einer Erdbeere h) meiner Karte

c) einem Wagen j) keinem Theater

d) einer Speisekarte k) keiner Wurst

f) meinem Hemd l) keinem Joghurt

g) meinem Hund

4) b) Frau Weber geht zur Bäckerei.

c) Der Kaffee ist auf dem Tisch.

d) Wir fahren zum Schloss.

e) Die Bibliothek ist gegenüber der Post.

f) Der Brief ist von der Frau.

g) Ist sie im Kino?

Page 122

1) False

2) a) False

b) True

3) a) False

b) True

4) a) Mein Hemd ist gelb. c) Die Jacken sind alt.

b) Der Rock ist groß. d) Die Erbsen sind grün.

5) a) das gelbe Hemd c) die alte Jacke

b) der große Rock d) die grüne Erbse

6) a) ein gelbes Hemd c) eine alte Jacke

b) ein großer Rock d) eine grüne Erbse

7) a) Sie e) Sie

b) du f) ihr

c) du g) du

d) Sie h) Sie

Page 129

1) a) Ich kaufe.

b) Ihr versteht Deutsch.

c) Sie kaufen Pizza.

d) Du fragst.

e) Wir spielen Fußball.

f) Er macht einen Fehler.

2) a) ich esse

er isst

wir essen

Sie essen

b) du fährst

wir fahren

ihr fahrt

c) du schläfst

er schläft

wir schlafen

ihr schlaft

Sie schlafen

3) a) du bist

er/sie/es ist

wir sind

ihr seid

Sie sind

b) ich habe

er/sie/es hat

ihr habt

Sie haben

4) b) Er geht aus. e) Sie kommen an.

c) Sie ruft an. f) Wir waschen ab.

d) Wir fahren ab.

5) a) Peter kann essen. c) Ich soll schreiben.

b) Sie mögen Hunde. d) Ich muss Tina besuchen.

Page 135-136

1) a) Italy d) His school

b) Went swimming e) Go hiking

c) Played table tennis f) At a campsite

2) a) Don't sing! e) Don't read!

b) Don't run! f) Don't listen!

c) Don't come! g) Don't sit!

d) Don't speak!

3) a) Singt! e) Geh!

b) Sprechen Sie nicht! f) Singen Sie nicht!

c) Seid ruhig! g) Komm!

d) Setzt euch! h) Geht nicht!

4) b) gefragt (asked) f) geschrieben (written)

c) gehört (listened) g) gesagt (said)

d) gegessen (eaten) h) gekauft (bought)

e) getrunken (drunk) i) gemacht (made / done)

5) Ich habe Fußball gespielt.

Ich habe gegessen.

Ich habe Milch gekauft.

Ich habe an Dieter geschrieben.

Ich habe Apfelsaft getrunken.

6) b) Ich fahre nächstes Jahr nach Spanien.

c) Du kommst nächste Woche hierhin.

d) Du machst das am Montag.

7) a) Ich werde am Samstag singen.

b) Er wird morgen besuchen.

c) Sie wird nächste Woche nach Spanien fahren.

d) Ich werde nächstes Jahr nach Portugal fahren.

e) Ich werde morgen putzen.

f) Sie werden morgen schlafen.

Page 145-146

1) b) Die Lampe ist nicht rot. (The lamp is not red.)

c) Ich habe keinen Bruder. (I have no brothers.)

d) Sie ist nicht meine Mutter. (She is not my mother.)

e) Bettina isst keinen Apfel. (Bettina eats no apples.)

2) a) Ich habe Hunger.

b) Morgen spiele ich Fußball.

c) Heute hast du kein Essen.

d) Samstags gehe ich ins Kino.

e) Ich trinke Tee.

f) Sie ist Berlinerin.

3) a) und d) oder

b) und e) aber

c) aber

4) 1b (weil = because)

2c (wenn = if)

3a (obwohl = although)

5) b) Ich koche nicht gern, obwohl Essen toll ist.

c) Ich habe Hunger, weil ich heute morgen Fußball gespielt habe.

d) Obwohl es neblig ist, spielt meine Mutter Fußball.

6) PRESENT TENSE — SPIELEN

du spielst

er/sie/es spielt

wir spielen

ihr spielt

sie spielen

PAST TENSE — KAUFEN

ich habe gekauft

er/sie/es hat gekauft

wir haben gekauft

Sie haben gekauft

sie haben gekauft

FUTURE TENSE — SCHWIMMEN

ich werde schwimmen

du wirst schwimmen

ihr werdet schwimmen

Sie werden schwimmen

sie werden schwimmen

PAST TENSE — FAHREN

ich bin gefahren

er/sie/es ist gefahren

wir sind gefahren

Sie sind gefahren

sie sind gefahren

7) THE DEFINITE ARTICLE

Nom.	der	die	das	die
Acc.	den	die	das	die
Dat.	dem	der	dem	den

KEIN, KEINE, KEIN

Nom.	kein	keine	kein	keine
Acc.	keinen	keine	kein	keine
Dat.	keinem	keiner	keinem	keinen

Track 1 Page 5

a)

: Es ist Viertel vor zwei.

b)

: Es beginnt um fünf nach drei.

c)

2: Es ist Viertel nach sieben.

d)

2: Der Supermarkt macht um halb sechs zu.

e)

1: Der Bus fährt um vier Uhr fünfunddreißig ab.

f)

M1: Treffen wir uns um zweiundzwanzig Uhr vierzig.

Track 2 Page 11

1) a)

F2: Wie geht es Ihnen, Frau Hoffmann?

F1: Sehr gut, danke.

b)

M1: Guten Morgen, Anton.

F2: Hallo Anton.

M2: Hallo! Darf ich euch meine Freundin Maria vorstellen?

c)

F2: Soll ich spülen?

M1: Ja, danke schön Susanna.

d)

M2: Möchtest du einen Kaffee, Flora?

F1: Nein danke, Herr Genzler, Kaffee trinke ich nie.

Track 3 Page 20

1)

M2: Wir sind fünf Personen in meiner Familie — mein Bruder, meine Stiefmutter, meine Großmutter, mein Vater und ich. Meine Großmutter hat eine schwarze Katze, die Kirsten heißt. Mein Vater und ich haben braune Haare und grüne Augen. Mein Bruder heißt Franz. Er ist ziemlich faul.

Track 4 Page 28

1) a)

M1: Ich bin Peter. Ich wohne in einer kleinen Wohnung in der Stadtmitte. Leider wohnen meine Freunde nicht in der Nähe.

b)

F2: Ich heiße Natalia. Unser Haus ist in einem Dorf. Es ist ein mittelgroßes Haus und ich wohne dort gern.

c)

M2: Ich bin Markus. Wir haben ein Haus am Meer in Norddeutschland. Ich wohne hier gern, weil es hier sehr schön ist.

d)

F1: Ich heiße Krista. Ich lebe hier gern, weil ich in den Bergen wohne und ich gern Ski fahre.

Track 5 Page 28

2)

F2: Ich stehe um halb sieben auf, ich wasche mich und ich frühstücke in der Küche. Bevor ich zur Schule gehe, muss ich mein Bett machen. Nachmittags mache ich meine Hausaufgaben. Mein Bruder deckt jeden Abend den Tisch. Er findet das langweilig.

Track 6 Page 33

1)

M1: Guten Tag, Frau Reinhard. Wie geht es Ihnen?

F1: Nicht so gut. Ich habe seit drei Tagen Halsschmerzen und ich huste auch viel.

M1: Machen Sie mal bitte den Mund auf. Ah, ja... Nehmen Sie dieses Medikament.

F1: Vielen Dank.

2)

M1: Guten Morgen, Herr Brand. Wie geht's?

M2: Nicht schlecht, aber mein Knie tut mir wirklich weh.

M1: Lassen Sie mich mal sehen. Ja, nehmen Sie diese Salbe dreimal am Tag.

M2: Vielen Dank, Herr Doktor.

3)

M1: Hallo Susanna. Wie geht's?

F2: Ich habe seit gestern Bauchschmerzen.

M1: Trink viel Wasser und iss keine Bonbons!

F2: Das ist so unfair, Herr Doktor!

Track 7 Page 40

1)

M1: Also, Maria, was ist dein Lieblingsfach?

F1: Mein Lieblingsfach ist Informatik, weil ich das einfach klasse finde! Ich hasse aber Musik — das ist so langweilig!

2)

M1: Und du, Gregor, was machst du gern?

M2: Erdkunde finde ich interessant, aber mein Lieblingsfach ist Geschichte. Ich mag Kunst nicht, weil ich nicht kreativ bin.

3)

M1: Kristina, was magst du nicht in der Schule?

F2: Ich hasse Mathe, weil das so schwierig ist, aber Englisch ist super, weil mein Lehrer toll ist.

Track 8 Page 44

1)

M2: Mein Name ist Stefan. Nächstes Jahr möchte ich Physik lernen, weil ich Ingenieur werden will. Mein Vater ist auch Ingenieur.

2)

F2: Ich heiße Lea. Ich möchte Französisch und Spanisch an der Uni studieren, weil ich Lehrerin oder Sekretärin werden möchte. Vielleicht werde ich im Ausland wohnen.

3)

M1: Ich bin Mario. Ich möchte Naturwissenschaften lernen, weil sie sehr interessant sind. Nach der Uni möchte ich Arzt oder Zahnarzt werden.

Track 9 Page 50

1) a)

M1: Entschuldigen Sie, wo ist die Bibliothek, bitte?

F1: Gehen Sie rechts, dann nehmen Sie die zweite Straße links. Die Bibliothek ist auf der linken Seite.

b)

M2: Entschuldigen Sie, wie komme ich bitte zum Schloss?

F1: Gehen Sie rechts, dann nehmen Sie die erste Straße links. Das Schloss ist am Ende der Straße.

c)

F2: Gibt es hier in der Nähe ein Kino?

F1: Ja. Gehen Sie hier links, dann gehen Sie geradeaus und das Kino ist auf der rechten Seite.

Track 10 Page 59

1) a)

M1: Guten Abend. Was möchten Sie essen?

F1: Ich hätte gern die Zwiebelsuppe.

M1: Ja, und als Hauptgericht?

F1: Ich nehme das Hähnchen mit Pommes.

b)

M1: Und für Sie?

F2: Keine Vorspeise für mich, danke. Als Hauptgericht möchte ich das Schweinefleisch mit Kartoffeln und ich nehme auch eine Cola, bitte.

c)

M1: Und für Sie?

M2: Also, zuerst möchte ich die Karottensuppe, das ist meine Lieblingssuppe! Dann nehme ich die Nudeln mit Meeresfrüchten und zum Trinken ein Glas Weißwein.

Track 11 Page 65

1)

F1: Guten Tag! Kann ich Ihnen helfen?

F2: Ja, ich möchte eine schwarze Hose, bitte.

F1: So, bitte schön.

F2: Nein, danke. Sie ist viel zu groß.

F1: Es tut mir leid, das ist die Letzte. Haben Sie noch einen Wunsch?

F2: Ich hätte gern noch einen roten Hut.

F1: Ja, hier ist einer.

F2: Ja, ich nehme ihn. Was kostet der?

F1: Fünfzehn Euro zwanzig.

F2: Danke schön.

Track 12 Page 72

1)

F1: Hallo, ich heiße Isabel. Ich gehe gern wandern und ab und zu fahre ich mit meinem Bruder Rad. Ich lese auch gern Romane.

2)

M2: Ich heiße Joshua. Ich gehe am Wochenende kegeln und ich sehe sehr gerne Filme im Fernsehen an. Am liebsten spiele ich Rugby.

3)

F2: Ich bin Olivia. Ich gehe nicht gern einkaufen, weil es so langweilig ist. Mein Lieblingshobby ist Schlittschuhlaufen.

Track 13 Page 80

1) a)

M1: Katrin, hast du Lust heute Abend ins Kino zu gehen?

F2: Es tut mir leid, Kurt. Ich muss meine Hausaufgaben machen.

b)

M1: Möchtest du morgen ins Schwimmbad gehen?

F2: Nein danke. Leider habe ich kein Geld.

c)

M1: Hast du Lust ins Theater zu gehen?

F2: Nein, Kurt, ich gehe nicht gern ins Theater.

d)

M1: Also, Katrin, möchtest du am Wochenende ins Restaurant gehen?

F1: Nein, ich kann nicht. Samstag fahre ich mit dem Zug nach Spanien.

Track 14 Page 80

2)

F1: Guten Morgen. Wie kann ich Ihnen helfen?

M2: Ich möchte bitte eine einfache Fahrkarte nach Frankfurt. Was kostet das?

F1: Das kostet zwanzig Euro neunzig.

M2: Wann fährt der nächste Zug?

F1: Der nächste Zug fährt in zehn Minuten ab.

M2: Von welchem Gleis fährt er ab?

F1: Von Gleis sieben.

M2: Vielen Dank.

F1: Bitte schön.

Track 15 Page 96

1)

M1: Guten Tag! Hier ist der europäische Wetterbericht für heute. In Frankreich ist es heute ziemlich kalt und sehr wolkig. In der Schweiz schneit es den ganzen Tag. In Belgien regnet es viel und in Holland ist es sehr windig. In Deutschland braucht man heute eine Sonnenbrille, weil es sonnig und heiß ist, aber in Österreich ist es neblig.

Track 16 Page 96

2)

F1: Hallo, Campingplatz Hirzberg. Wie kann ich Ihnen helfen?

M2: Hallo, ich möchte bitte einen Platz für einen Wohnwagen reservieren.

F1: Wie lange wollen Sie bleiben?

M2: Vom vierten bis elften August.

F1: Also, sieben Nächte. Leider haben wir nur vom vierten August für vier Nächte Platz. Geht das?

M2: Ja, das geht. Was kostet das bitte? Wir sind zwei Erwachsene und zwei Kinder, und wir haben auch eine Katze.

F1: Das kostet dreißig Euro pro Nacht. Die Katze ist kostenlos.

Track 17 Page 122

1)

M1: Meine Freundin Carola ist größer als Bernd. Sie ist 1,65 Meter groß. Carola ist aber jünger als Bernd, der vierzehn ist.

2)

F2: Meine Freundin Katja ist die Kleinste in ihrer Familie. Sie hat drei ältere Brüder. Ihr Bruder Georg ist der Älteste.

3)

M2: Sonja hat kürzere Haare als Andrea, und ihr Auto ist viel schneller als Andreas Auto. Andrea hat aber eine größere Wohnung.

Track 18 Page 135

1)

M1: Letztes Jahr bin ich mit meiner Familie nach Italien geflogen. Das Wetter war so schön — jeden Tag ist es sonnig gewesen. Meine Mutter ist schwimmen gegangen und mein Bruder und ich, wir haben Tischtennis gespielt. Nächstes Jahr fahre ich mit meiner Schule in die Schweiz. Wir werden wandern gehen und auf einem Campingplatz übernachten.

Index

Index

DHS31